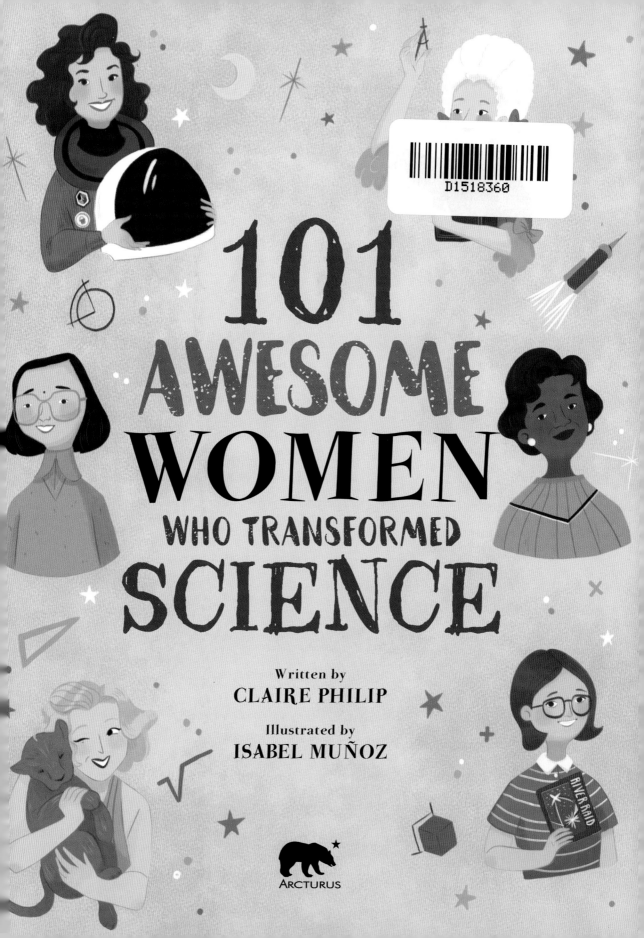

101 AWESOME WOMEN WHO TRANSFORMED SCIENCE

Written by
CLAIRE PHILIP

Illustrated by
ISABEL MUÑOZ

ARCTURUS

This edition published in 2020
by Arcturus Publishing Limited
26/27 Bickels Yard, 151–153 Bermondsey Street,
London SE1 3HA

Copyright © Arcturus Holdings Limited

All rights reserved. No part of this publication
may be reproduced, stored in a retrieval
system, or transmitted, in any form or by any
means, electronic, mechanical, photocopying,
recording or otherwise, without prior written
permission in accordance with the provisions
of the Copyright Act 1956 (as amended). Any
person or persons who do any unauthorised
act in relation to this publication may be liable
to criminal prosecution and civil claims for
damages.

Author: Claire Philip
Illustrator: Isabel Muñoz
Designer: Sally Bond
Editor: Donna Gregory

ISBN: 978-1-78888-376-4
CH006568NT

Supplier 42, Date 1119, Print run 8268

Printed in Singapore

CONTENTS

INTRODUCTION

This compendium is a celebration of the groundbreaking achievements of 101 incredible female scientists, without whom our world would be a very different place. Many of these women lived in historical periods when the obstacles to their work would have seemed insurmountable. But that didn't hold back these brave pioneers! They flew in the face of societal expectations, financial and legal barriers, ignorance, and prejudice. When times were tough and pay was low (or nonexistent) they persevered because they believed in their cause, their abilities, and their strength to create change. They never gave up on their

MARGUERITE CATHERINE PEREY (PAGE 72)

dreams, regardless of the odds. Many of these women's contributions to science were downplayed or overlooked during their own lifetime—or even credited to male colleagues. We can now finally correct this injustice, and acknowledge the importance of their work, while standing in awe of their discipline and determination, and their willingness to think big in the face of societal small-mindedness.

One area of science in which women have always been involved is medicine, whether as midwives or healers. However, for many years, the best place for women to learn about other areas of science was in a convent.

MARIA MARGARETHA KIRCH (PAGE 17)

Universities were limited to men until just a few hundred years ago. In the eighteenth century, more women entered the scientific arena, yet they were still at a great disadvantage. This didn't hold back our heroines, however, and slowly but surely there was more acceptance of their contributions, as the efforts and results of female scientists became impossible to ignore.

Once women had full access to education, their numbers slowly increased and there were more openings for paid, respectable careers in science. In this collection, we delve into the fields of engineering, medicine, astronomy, technology, mathematics, and chemistry, revealing women's lives that would be worthy of amazing blockbuster movie adaptations.

Today, women have more opportunity than ever before to make a difference to the future of world. However, thanks to the changes in technology, society, and the environment, we also face greater challenges than we did in the past. Now, more than ever, we need bright young women to take their place in the world's laboratories, and to think creatively about how to make the Earth a better, safer place. We need adventurous explorers tempted by space travel, and brilliant problem solvers who can solve the global medical emergencies of the future. Thanks to the emphasis on STEM (science, technology, engineering, and mathematics) in schools today, inspiration is all around us. The future is bright for women—so read on, and meet some of the most inspiring characters we know of. Turn the page, and get inspired!

DOROTHY JOHNSON VAUGHAN (PAGE 78)

VIRGINIA APGAR (PAGE 71)

MERIT PTAH
Doctor

*c.*2700–2650 BCE

Merit Ptah was born around 2700 BCE in ancient Egypt during the Second Dynasty (*c.*2890–*c.*2686 BCE). She is the first female doctor in history (and all of science) that we know by name!

At her grave she is named as the royal chief physician to the country's leader, the pharaoh, who was revered as a god on Earth. As well as treating the monarch, it is likely that she would have taught and overseen many other doctors, including men, as they studied and treated their patients.

Lots of women in ancient Egypt held highly important positions, so it was not unusual for Merit Ptah to rise to such an influential role in the court. We know that women regularly became physicians and midwives—one

EGYPTIAN JAR

example being Pesehet (born *c.*2500 BCE). She was given the title of "Lady Overseer of Female Physicians." She was born after Merit Ptah, but we know less about her medical role.

The physicians of ancient Egypt had a good understanding of human anatomy (for the time), thanks in part to the practice of mummification (the preparation of the body for the afterlife). They observed how the major organs worked and learned how to heal the body using a mixture of spiritual ceremonies and basic plant-based medicine.

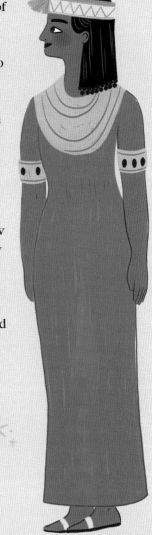

ATHIRTE
ASTRONOMER

c.1900–1840 BCE

Astronomy (the study of stars, comets, planets, and galaxies), was an important part of life in many ancient cultures—including Egypt, where a woman named Athirte was particularly famed for her talent and skill in reading the night sky.

Born around 1900 BCE, she was the daughter of a pharaoh named Sesostris. Athirte became well known for her dedication to calculating the positions of the planets and was highly praised for her supreme intellect and intuition.

Her father claimed that she was "very clever in the knowledge of the future," and he relied on her understanding of the stars to predict future events—it seems that her observations were often correct!

Ancient civilizations relied heavily on reading signs from the natural world to predict important events throughout the year. By observing the heavens, it was noted by the ancient Egyptians that the great flooding of the River Nile always occurred around the time of the summer solstice, just after the star Sirius was high in the sky. This awareness allowed them to successfully predict and plan their agricultural year and thrive for thousands of years.

EGYPTIAN CALENDAR

AGNODICE
DOCTOR

4th century BCE

Agnodice, from Athens, Greece, is famed for being one of the first female doctors. According to legend, she dressed up as a man in order to become a doctor. This was a huge risk for her, as it was illegal for women to study medicine at this time. Once she had qualified, she continued using her disguise and utilized her expertise by treating women in childbirth. After eventually revealing her gender and identity, the laws were changed so that women could be treated by female physicians.

We do not know for certain if she was a real historical figure or a myth, yet her story is an important one. She represents the right for women everywhere to work in medicine—and the right for women to have a female doctor.

AGLAONIKE
Astronomer

1st or 2nd century BCE

Aglaonike was born in Thessaly, Greece, and is one of the earliest female astronomers that we know of. She studied the night sky in the ancient civilization of Mesopotamia and through careful observation, learned all about the movements of the moon and how it moved through its phases.

At that time, this kind of knowledge gave her a huge amount of power, making it likely that she became an important member of society. The general public didn't understand the wonders of space and were afraid of the unknown. This meant that she may also have been regarded as a sorceress— even a witch. Her impeccable ability to accurately predict seemingly random events, such as lunar eclipses, was sometimes distrusted … after all, if she knew about the heavens, what else did she know?

HYPATIA
Mathematician

c.350–415 CE

The daughter of the keeper of the Great Library of Alexandria in Egypt, Hypatia was born into an exciting ancient world of mathematic and scientific discovery.

She excelled in her studies, taking after her father, and eventually became a renowned philosopher and teacher in her own right. As well as writing her own mathematical works, Hypatia lectured on the works of Plato and Aristotle, attracting people from far and wide to hear her speak.

Unfortunately, many of Hypatia's ideas were not compatible with the Christian dogmas of the time. Her intelligence and influence made her a threat to the leaders of the day, and she was unfairly scapegoated as a reason for unrest in Alexandria. Soon after, she was murdered, yet her memory lives on as a symbol of great female intellect.

TROTA OF SALERNO
MEDICAL SCIENTIST

c.1030–1097

For many thousands of years, women were subjected to all kinds of bizarre medical treatments based on Galen's theory of humorism. Female health was widely misunderstood, so many of the "cures" that doctors advised simply didn't work.

Trota, a woman from Salerno in the south of Italy, used her knowledge of healing and wrote *The Trotula*, a group of highly practical texts, based on her experiences and understanding of female health.

This text finally helped women with their ailments. Trota successfully demonstrated to the world that women could be excellent authorities on health, and that often, simply observing and listening to the body is the best way forward. Her medical texts influenced the world for hundreds of years.

SAINT HILDEGARD OF BINGEN
POLYMATH

1098–1179

LAVENDER

Hildegard of Bingen has been described as one of the most powerful women of the late middle ages. Born in Germany in 1098, she was both a mystic and a scientist. In her lifetime she founded two successful monasteries and, in 2012, she was named a Doctor of the Church by Pope Benedict XVI.

Her early childhood years were somewhat unusual. Her parents chose to send her into a life of confinement at a monastery, where, from a very early age, she began to have prophetic visions.

These would leave her exhausted, yet gave her great insight. She slowly gained confidence in sharing her revelations with her superiors in the church. They were very impressed by her understanding of both religion and humanity.

Historians have noted that she was particularly good at taking symbols from her imagination and using logical reasoning to apply her ideas to the world around her.

"Wisdom teaches in the light of love, and bids me tell how I was brought into this my gift of vision ..."

As well as her intuitive medical understanding, she had a great musical talent, composing many songs and chants, and even a morality play called *Ordo Virtutum*.

Hildegard toured, preached, and wrote extensively over the years, showing herself to be a highly capable female leader of the day.

In the sixteenth century, hundreds of years after her death, the Catholic church chose to make her a saint—a process that was concluded in 2012. Her teachings showed the world how deep a woman's insight could be, and her spiritual ideas continue to spark discussion all these centuries later.

This skill led her to writing prolifically and gaining approval by the Pope. He encouraged her to write more on natural sciences, and as a result, she became the first German female physician.

She was especially interested in the use of tinctures, believing that with plants and precious stones, Earth provides everything humans need to heal.

HILDEGARD'S MAP OF THE UNIVERSE

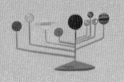

IN FOCUS
Women in Astronomy

Some of the most exciting—and important— discoveries about our universe were made by women. Often they went unacknowledged at the time, but here we celebrate their incredible contributions to science.

From ancient times, women as well as men have looked to the stars in wonder—and for answers. Imagine looking up at the night sky and seeing star upon star studded against a black blanket … then one night witnessing a comet blazing against the darkness. You'd be amazed, and desperate to know more about the world above.

Though there are few records from thousands of years ago, we do know that astronomy was important in many ancient cultures. In ancient Egypt, Athirte dedicated her life to calculating the positions of the planets. She was so in tune with their movements that it was thought she could predict future events as the planets affected Earth.

SOPHIA BRAHE (PAGE 14)

From the sixteenth century, astronomers such as Sophia Brahe, with her brother Tycho Brahe, began making more and more accurate astronomical calculations

(she was able to help him predict a lunar eclipse). And in the eighteenth century, Caroline Herschel became the first professional female astronomer. She was also the first woman to find a comet (her first of eight). She was made an honorary member of the then all-male Royal Astronomical Society, a huge accomplishment.

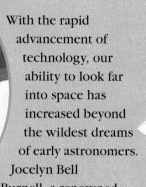

CAROLINE HERSCHEL (PAGE 24)

With the rapid advancement of technology, our ability to look far into space has increased beyond the wildest dreams of early astronomers. Jocelyn Bell Burnell, a renowned astrophysicist, jointly made one of the greatest astronomical discoveries of the last hundred years. She identified pulsars—rotating neutron stars that appear to pulse—using an incredibly powerful telescope that revealed the far reaches of space.

These women have paved the way for girls today, and the future is star-bright for those who want to study space and all its precious mysteries.

ANNIE JUMP CANNON (PAGE 44)

In the early twentieth century, Annie Jump Cannon, the "census taker of the sky," spoke out for women's rights and the discrepancies she saw. Annie discovered more than 300 stars herself, and her work was instrumental in the development of star classification.

JOCELYN BELL BURNELL (PAGE 108)

SOPHIA BRAHE
Astronomer

1556–1643

SOLAR ECLIPSE

Sophia Brahe, a talented Scandinavian researcher and writer, is the somewhat lesser-known sister of famous astronomer Tycho Brahe, the man whose astronomical calculations led to the understanding of planetary motion.

Her brother described her as having an "animus invictus," a "determined mind," and this is certainly shown in her life. She relentlessly studied horticulture, chemistry, medicine, and even astronomy, despite the fact that studying the sky was frowned upon by her noble family.

SEXTANT

Sophia even assisted her brother at his observatory on island in the sea between Denmark and Sweden, and she was with him in November 1572 when he discovered a new star in the constellation Cassiopea. It is also documented that she helped him calculate and predict a lunar eclipse the following year.

Sophia demonstrated her capabilities in many areas of life, running her first husband's estate after his death and

"When Denmark remembers her son Tycho, she should not forget the noble woman who in spirit more than blood was his sister. That shining star on our Danish sky was indeed a double star!"

JOHAN RUNEBERG

SOPHIA'S DOG

constructing exceptionally beautiful gardens. Her medical knowledge and intuition was also impressive, studying the potential use of small doses of poison as medicine.

Sophia became engaged to her second husband, Erik Lange, a nobleman fascinated with alchemy, in 1590. Their relationship was fraught with poverty and they were separated for much of their engagement. Sadly, he too died young, yet after his death she continued working. She went on to write extensively on the genealogy of 60 Danish noble families, creating a highly important historical document.

ELISABETH HEVELIUS
Astronomer

1647–1693

Nicknamed "the mother of moon charts," Elisabeth Hevelius was born into a rich merchant family in the mid-1600s. Like other well educated women in Gdańsk, Poland, she was formally educated and likely fluent in multiple languages, including Latin.

At a young age, she married the astronomer Johannes Hevelius, the owner of possibly the best observatory in the world at that time and one of the earliest astronomers to map the moon and name its features.

She helped her much older husband in his observations, and developed her own studies of astronomy, developing a great talent for observing celestial bodies.

After Johannes' death, she published two collections of her husband's work, one of which was *Prodromus astronomiae*, a catalogue and atlas of more than 1500 stars. Compiling and presenting this amount of information alone was an enormous scientific feat.

Elisabeth's dedication to astronomy and the documentation of the information that she and her husband discovered shows how determined female scientists can be, and what they can achieve.

"A complimentary remark was always made about Madam Hevelius, who was the first woman, to my knowledge, who was not frightened to face the fatigue of making astronomical observations and calculations."

FRANÇOIS ARAGO

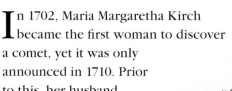

MARIA MARGARETHA KIRCH
ASTRONOMER

1670–1720

In 1702, Maria Margaretha Kirch became the first woman to discover a comet, yet it was only announced in 1710. Prior to this, her husband Gottfried Kirch was credited with the find.

Maria worked closely with Gottfried, who was the astronomer royal at the court of King Frederick I in Berlin, Germany, for many years. They functioned very well as a team, making observations and complex calculations to produce detailed calendars of the night sky.

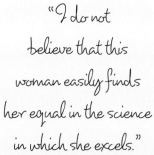

"I do not believe that this woman easily finds her equal in the science in which she excels."

GOTTFRIED LEIBNIZ

In her youth she was well educated, first by her father, then her uncle, and also the astronomer Christoph Arnold. Later in life, she published observations on the northern lights and wrote papers on the conjunctions of the Sun with various planets.

Despite her clear talent and ability, after her husband's death Maria struggled to find recognition for her skill. She persevered by petitioning for a position as an assistant astronomer, yet the local scientific community refused her request and rejected her prominence.

THE NORTHERN LIGHTS

They were not ready to set a precedent for other female scientists to enter the male dominated realm of astronomy, despite her background.

ÉMILIE DU CHÂTELET

MATHEMATICIAN

1706–1749

É milie du Châtelet from France is one of the most glamorous mathematicians of all time. She is often remembered for her love affair with the famous Enlightenment philosopher and writer Voltaire, yet she was a highly astute intellectual in her own right.

She openly supported education of women, and reportedly stated that if she was king, she would "reform an abuse which effectively cuts back half of humanity … I would have women participate in all human rights, and above all, those of the mind."

"I used to teach myself with you. But now you have flown up where I can no longer follow."

VOLTAIRE AFTER ÉMILIE'S DEATH

Throughout her childhood she was encouraged to learn, and by the age of twelve was fluent in German, Italian, Latin, and Greek.

She married young, at just eighteen years old, to Marquis Florent-Claude du Chastellet, an army officer of high regard. Her husband was often away from home on duty, which allowed Émilie to study science and mathematics in her own time, as well as spend

DEVICE TO SHOW GALILEO'S LAW OF MOTION

NEWTON'S SECOND LAW OF MOTION

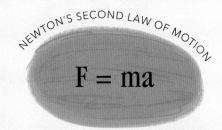

$$F = ma$$

time with Voltaire, who celebrated her intelligence and with whom she renovated their estate, including the library, which held thousands of books—reportedly more than 20,000 titles.

Her greatest achievement was her commentary and translation of Sir Isaac Newton's influential work, *Principia Mathematica*, one of the most important works in the history of scientific thought. It has been said that not only did she convert Newton's ideas into French— she made them understandable.

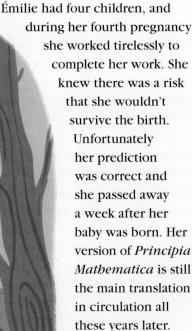

Émilie had four children, and during her fourth pregnancy she worked tirelessly to complete her work. She knew there was a risk that she wouldn't survive the birth. Unfortunately her prediction was correct and she passed away a week after her baby was born. Her version of *Principia Mathematica* is still the main translation in circulation all these years later.

LAURA BASSI
Professor of Anatomy and Philosophy

1711–1778

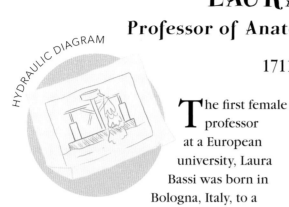

HYDRAULIC DIAGRAM

The first female professor at a European university, Laura Bassi was born in Bologna, Italy, to a wealthy lawyer. She was an incredibly intelligent child and her love of learning was noticed by Cardinal Prospero Lambertini, who would later become the pope.

At the age of just 21, she was appointed as a professor of anatomy, and two years later, a professor of philosophy at the university of Bologna. This was revolutionary, yet Laura was still sidelined, and had to teach classes in her own home.

Laura married Guiseppe Varetti, also an academic, and had many children with him, yet she did not give up her love for science. They set up research facilities and fervently studied both physics and electricity together, attracting students throughout Europe.

In 1745, Laura Bassi joined a group of academics set up by Lambertini. For many years she researched a plethora of topics, including hydraulics.

In 1776 she was made the Chair of Experimental Physics. Not only did this make her the first woman to hold such a position, she was also paid properly for it. At the end of her career she was the highest-paid lecturer at Bologna university, paving the way for other female academics to follow in her footsteps.

" Laura Bassi [was] the first woman in the history of the world to hold an academic chair. And not only to hold it, but to earn a salary proportionate to her duties— by the end of her career she was the highest-paid lecturer in the entire university."

DALE DEBAKCSY

MARIA GAETANA AGNESI

Mathematician

1718–1799

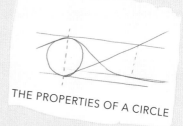

THE PROPERTIES OF A CIRCLE

Maria Gaetana Agnesi was born into a wealthy Italian family in 1718, and benefited from many highly esteemed tutors as she grew up. Although she has been described as a child prodigy, she also seems to have been a reluctant intellect, preferring a quiet life away from the limelight.

It is said that by the age of 11, she had mastered Italian, French, Latin, German, Greek, Hebrew, and Spanish. There are accounts of her delivering an impressive speech in Latin about the rights of women to study "the fine arts and the sublime sciences" to her father's friends as a mid-teenager. At the age of 20, however, she informed her father that she would prefer a life of religious devotion.

While she didn't enter the church, she certainly maintained a life of little extravagance. She was encouraged to study mathematics, however, and wrote a textbook to teach the subject to her younger brothers and sisters.

This work, the *Instituzioni analitiche ad uso della gioventù italiana* was printed in 1748 and brought Maria widespread recognition, receiving an invitation from Pope Benedict XIV to become an honorary reader at the University of Bologna.

Maria, however, still longed for a quiet life, and eventually became a nun, dedicating her time and resources to charity.

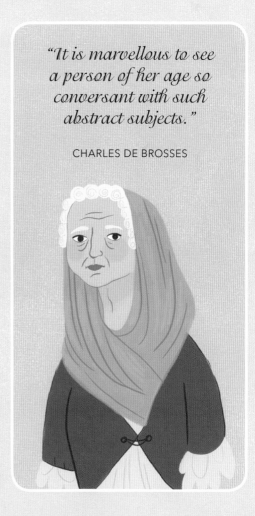

"It is marvellous to see a person of her age so conversant with such abstract subjects."

CHARLES DE BROSSES

CATHERINE CHARLOTTE DE LA GARDIE

Vaccination Pioneer

1723–1763

Born into Swedish nobility, Catherine Charlotte de La Gardie became the lady-in-waiting to Princess Lovisa Ulrika in 1744, before marrying a count in 1748.

An incredibly open-minded, brave woman of her day, Catherine was a keen supporter of the age of Enlightenment—a period of great political, philosophical, and scientific overhaul.

SPREADING THE NEWS

She is famous for publicly vaccinating her children against the deadly smallpox disease during a terrible outbreak, as well as encouraging local poorer woman to do the same. At this time, inoculations were greatly resisted, so her act of confidence in the

SMALLPOX

new medicine led others to follow suit, most likely saving many lives.

Catherine is also remembered for stopping the last witch trial in Sweden. In 1757, eighteen people were arrested and about to go on trial for witchcraft, despite the fact that such accusations were becoming outdated. She was able to intervene in the legal process, preventing the innocent parties from further torture, as well as

SMALLPOX WAS A WIDESPREAD DISEASE IN THE EIGHTEENTH CENTURY. IN SWEDEN, IT WAS SAID TO HAVE CAUSED THE DEATH OF 300,000 PEOPLE BETWEEN 1750 AND 1800. 95 PERCENT OF THOSE WERE PROBABLY CHILDREN.

organize compensation for them—their terrible treatment meant that they were unable to work. The accused were released without charge and Catherine was hailed as a heroine.

Catherine's sister-in-law was also an important figure in the world of science,

Countess Eva Ekeblad developed methods to distill and make flour from potatoes, which contributed to the reduction of devastating famines at that time. She was the first woman allowed entry to the Royal Swedish Academy of Sciences.

CAROLINE HERSCHEL

ASTRONOMER

1750–1848

Caroline Herschel was born in Hanover (now Germany) in 1750. She was the first professional female astronomer.

In her early years she had to tend to household duties. She was only able to leave home and join her brother, William, in England after he promised his mother to pay for a maid to replace her.

At first, she spent much of her time singing in his concerts—he was a keen musician—yet soon William's interest shifted to astronomy.

Caroline joined him in this new obsession and learned mathematics and science. She assisted him as he worked and helped record observations from his telescopes, undertaking many complex calculations from the findings.

She also helped him build the telescopes—their house had a room for grinding the shape of the mirrors, as well as polishing the glass.

William discovered the planet later named Uranus in 1781 after initially thinking it was a comet. He was awarded the role of royal astronomer to King George III soon after this monumental find.

Uranus was the first planet to have been discovered since Saturn, thousands of years before, so William became famous immediately.

Brother and sister worked together for many years, surveying and cataloguing the sky

URANUS

COMET

"Caroline Herschel's legacy is undoubtedly lasting. There are not only the discoveries in themselves, she was also incredibly meticulous in cataloguing and recordering her discoveries, and in the transcription of astronomical data."

SHERRY SUYU

to discover more than 2000 nebulae and stars. Caroline herself was the first woman to find a comet (she found eight in total).

She was eventually given a salary by King George for her role as her brother's assistant, being paid £50 (approx. US$ 65) annually. Later, she was further rewarded by being made an honorary member of the Royal Astronomical Society in England for her contribution to astronomy—an amazing accomplishment as it was an all-male group at the time.

Caroline Herschel is rightly remembered for her own dedication to the science of astronomy and deserves the recognition and high praise she is awarded.

JANE MARCET

Chemist

1769–1858

Jane Marcet, the first female science writer, wrote a series of best-selling science books. Her most famous work is called *Conversations on Chemistry*, and it was anonymously published in 1806 to wide acclaim.

"No one at this time can duly estimate the importance of Mrs. Marcet's scientific works."

MARY SOMERVILLE

Jane was born in London to a wealthy banker and was home-schooled to a high level.

She married Alexander Marcet, a political exile from Switzerland and a physician with a great interest in chemistry. Together, they carried out experiments at their home.

This innovative book taught the fundamentals of chemistry by explaining key concepts through conversations between two young female students and their teacher.

Jane believed that public opinion was against the idea that girls should study science. She showed through her characters how willing young girls were to learn. After attending lectures by eminent chemist Humphry Davy, she set to write a text to demonstrate this.

She went on to write more influential books, including *Conversations on Political Economy*, which explained the complex ideas of economists such as Adam Smith.

Jane was part of an intellectual circle in London and immersed herself in learning. Her works became successful because she was able to present science in a way that was approachable and understandable—and available to the poor.

Michael Faraday, the son of a blacksmith, and later a hugely influential scientist, read her books and quoted them as the foundation for his learning.

SARAH GUPPY

INVENTOR

1770–1852

Exercise Bed

Sarah Guppy was a prolific female inventor who lived during the Industrial Revolution. She was born in Birmingham, England, to a wealthy family and later married a trader from Bristol.

CLIFTON SUSPENSION BRIDGE

Sarah and her husband became part of a circle of leading figures of the day, which included Isambard Kingdom Brunel, the creator of the Great Western Railway—the train line that linked London to Bristol. Sarah was interested in the engineering problems posed by bridges, and made significant contributions to the design of several major projects. She made models of the Clifton Suspension Bridge for Brunel, and patented a system of piling to anchor bridges properly and stop them from being washed away by floods or erosion.

She is widely known for her inventions and innovative engineering ideas, as well as being a campaigner, writer, and esteemed buisiness woman Sarah seems to have loved coming up with ideas, and has even been credited with the curious invention of a machine that can make breakfast, and a bed that can be used for exercise!

Sarah was a prolific letter-writer and had strong ideas about animal welfare and town planning—she lobbied the Earl of Liverpool to close Smithfield Market, where animals were herded though the streets in a dreadful condition.

"There are no statues of Sarah Guppy, no plaques that recount her inventions. In our culture, it [is] acceptable for women and their achievements to be buried, covered over, dismissed."

RACHEL BENTHAM AND ALYSON HALLETT

SOPHIE GERMAIN

Mathematician

1776–1831

Sophie Germain was a revolutionary female mathematician born in France in 1776. She lived at home her entire life and never married, yet dedicated herself to her studies with great passion.

Early biographies state that her parents disagreed with how much she immersed herself in their extensive library, so she would read at night by candlelight to be undetected, teaching herself both Latin and Greek. She couldn't be stopped, however, and when Sophie was eighteen she found a way to read the lecture notes from the male-only École Polytechnique.

She wrote an end of term paper and submitted it, pretending to be a male student at the school. Her work impressed the teacher so much that he when he discovered she was the author, he offered to oversee her learning. After, Sophie corresponded with other great mathematicians, such as Carl Gauss who was nicknamed the prince

of mathematics, initially using a male pseudonym in case her true identity was rejected.

Gauss was enthralled by her abilities, and is quoted as saying: "How can I describe my astonishment and admiration on seeing my esteemed

correspondent M. Le Blanc metamorphosed into this celebrated person … when a woman, because of her sex, our customs and prejudices, encounters infinitely more obstacles than men familiarising herself with … problems, yet overcomes these fetters and penetrates that which is most hidden, she doubtless has the most noble courage, extraordinary talent, and superior genius."

In the early 1800s, the French Academy of Sciences offered a prize to anyone able to provide a mathematical explanation of an experiment about vibrating plates. Sophie tried to explain it—yet despite her clear determination, lacked enough mathematical understanding at that time. She failed on both her first and second attempts, but eventually won the

"It matters little who first arrives at an idea, rather what is significant is how far that idea can go."

prize on her third try after years of study and correspondence with experts in the field. Sadly, because she was a woman, Sophie was not celebrated widely for her achievements.

Sophie also made impressive contributions toward establishing proof of one of the most complex mathematical problems of the day— Fermat's last theorem.

In 1816 she was awarded a prize from the French Academy for her work on elasticity. Her theory explained the patterns that sand formed when placed on vibrating elastic surfaces. This information was used in the construction of the Eiffel Tower.

Before her death, aged 55, she received a degree from the University of Gottingen in recognition of her excellent contributions.

$$X^n + y^n = Z^n$$

FERMAT'S LAST THEOREM

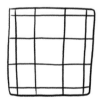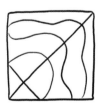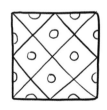

PATTERNS CAUSED BY VIBRATING PLATES

MARIA DALLE DONNE
DOCTOR

1778–1842

Maria Dalle Donne was the first woman to receive a doctorate (the highest level of degree) in medicine. Her achievements and career are remarkable—not only because of her academic contributions at a time when opportunities for women were so limited—but also due to her extremely humble beginnings.

She was born to a very poor peasant family that lived in a village outside of Bologna, yet her cleverness was picked up from an early age and she was encouraged to study at the local, highly esteemed university.

In 1799 she passed the medical exams with the highest possible grade, and one year later published scientific papers, one on the female reproductive system, one on female fertility, and one on midwifery.

We don't have many details about her career, yet we do know that she was dedicated to midwifery for many decades: in 1804 she was made the director of the school for midwives, and in 1832 she became the Director of the Department of Midwifery at Bologna University.

"Exceptionally talented and intelligent."

LAURA LYNN WINDSOR

MARY SOMERVILLE
MATHEMATICIAN AND ASTRONOMER

1780–1872

Mary Somerville was a Scottish mathematician, astronomer, and science writer. She and Caroline Herschel were the first female members of the Royal Astronomical Society, and she was an avid promoter of women's rights.

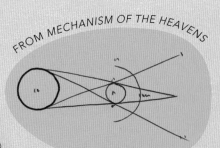

FROM MECHANISM OF THE HEAVENS

MARINE PHOSPHORESCENCE

first ever paper written by a woman to be published by the Royal Society, and in 1827 she translated and explained the mathematical work of Laplace, an eminent French scholar in a volume called *The Mechanism of the Heavens*.

She reportedly became interested in mathematics as a teenager, yet her family and first husband gave her little encouragement. It was only when she remarried after her husband's death, that her studies were supported.

Her work, "The magnetic properties of the violet rays of the solar spectrum," was the

"I ... thought it unjust that women should have been given a desire for knowledge if it were wrong to acquire it."

After her second book was published in 1834, she was elected to join the Royal Astronomical Society and was awarded a large pension by the King. Her two further books, *Physical Geography* and *Molecular and Microscopic Science* were used as educational resources for many years.

ANNA ATKINS

Botanist

1799–1871

Originally trained as a botanist (an expert in the study of plants), Anna Atkins is famous for being a pioneer in the world of photography, and is considered by many as the first female photographer.

She is known for creating more than 10,000 images to illustrate a book of botanical specimens called *Photographs of British Algae: Cyanotype Impressions*.

Anna's father, John George Children, was the secretary of the Royal Society and a scientist. Through his connections, he learned of the photographic processes that were currently being invented, and introduced them to his daughter, who helped him in his lab as an assistant.

CYANOTYPE IMPRESSIONS

Anna had hand-drawn many illustrations for her father's first book and so was naturally intrigued at this new way of making images. She became particularly interested in cyanotypes, which are commonly known as sun prints.

Here, the item to be captured is placed on special paper and exposed to sunlight. After being washed in water, the areas that were uncovered turn blue (hence the term blueprint).

Anna had learned about this cyanotype printing method through the renowned chemist and astronomer Sir John Herschel, who just so happened to be a friend of the family. He had developed the method of recording images in 1842.

Her beautiful book is full of white outlines of algae, contrasted against deep blue backgrounds, and is both an example of female innovation and determined focus, and a treasury of nature.

"The difficulty of making accurate drawings of objects so minute
as many of the Algae and Confervae has induced me to avail
myself of Sir John Herschel's beautiful process of Cyanotype,
to obtain impressions of the plants themselves, which I have
much pleasure in offering to my botanical friends."

FLORENCE NIGHTINGALE
Nurse and Mathematician

1820–1910

FLORENCE'S OWL

The world's most famous nurse, Florence Nightingale changed the world of medicine. She was born in Italy in 1820 while her wealthy English parents were on their honeymoon, and she enjoyed a privileged upbringing.

Florence surprised her parents as a teenager by announcing that she wanted to become a nurse. They didn't approve at first—at the start of the nineteenth century, nurses had to work without training or basic pay, and working conditions in hospitals were terrible. It was not seen as the profession of a lady!

Eventually, Florence's father William gave in. He saw how determined his daughter was and, in 1851, allowed her to study nursing in

Germany at a Christian school. It was here that she learned the importance of hospital cleanliness for patients, as well as how to care

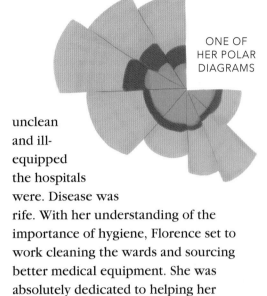

ONE OF
HER POLAR
DIAGRAMS

for them. On her return to England, Florence applied her knowledge and by 1853 was running a successful hospital in London as lady superintendent.

"I attribute my success to this—I never gave or took any excuse."

It wasn't long after, in 1854, that the Crimean War broke out. British troops were sent to the Crimea in south Russia (now part of Ukraine) and soon news of how bad the conditions were for injured soldiers reached London.

Florence was asked to take a team of nurses to Crimea by the Minister for War, Sidney Herbert, and when they arrived she was shocked by how unclean and ill-equipped the hospitals were. Disease was rife. With her understanding of the importance of hygiene, Florence set to work cleaning the wards and sourcing better medical equipment. She was absolutely dedicated to helping her patients, checking on them at night by lamplight, and even reportedly writing letters on behalf of wounded soldiers. The war lasted two years, and when she returned, Florence was seen as a national heroine.

After the war, Queen Victoria herself thanked her for her efforts and took her advice on how to improve army hospitals. Florence didn't rest—she wrote and published a book called *Notes on Nursing*, founded the Nightingale School and Home for Nurses, and continued to encourage the development of nursing and hygiene in hospitals. Florence was also made the first female member of the Royal Statistical Society—her statistic-based graphics showed how improvements in hygiene could save lives.

Her work still impacts the medical world today.

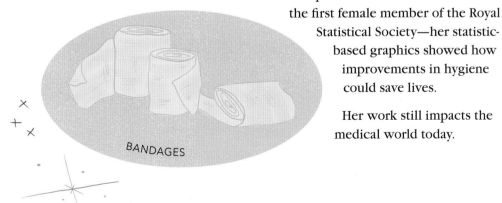

BANDAGES

ELIZABETH BLACKWELL

DOCTOR

1821–1910

Elizabeth Blackwell was the first woman to qualify as a doctor in America, and changed the face of medical care for women.

She was born in Bristol, England, in 1821, and immigrated with her family to America aged 11. After her father, an anti-slavery activist, passed away, she set up a school with her sisters to provide the family with money.

Elizabeth soon developed an interest in medicine and decided to become a physician. A close family friend had suffered during an illness, and had commented that she would have had more sympathetic treatment if her doctor had been a woman.

This got Elizabeth thinking. She applied to medical schools, yet was only granted admission to one—the Geneva Medical College in New York. It was an all-male establishment and its students were allowed to vote on whether Elizabeth could attend. It is said that they voted her in as a joke. Elizabeth wasn't granted the same equal treatment as her male peers, but she earned their respect by demonstrating her abilities and intellect.

After she qualified, Elizabeth went on to have an incredible career on both sides of the Atlantic. She worked in America,

"The idea of winning a doctor's degree gradually assumed the aspect of a great moral struggle, and the moral fight possessed immense attraction for me."

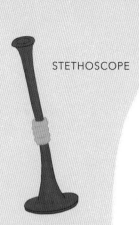

STETHOSCOPE

London, and Paris and continued her medical studies by learning midwifery. Sadly she contracted an eye condition, causing her to lose sight in one eye and removing her ability to train to become a surgeon. Not to be discouraged, in 1857 she opened the New York Infirmary for Indigent Women and Children, and in 1868 opened a medical school for women at her hospital.

Elizabeth was determined that women should have the same right as men to study medicine and become medical professionals, and she founded the National Health Society in 1871 as a means to educate the public about health. Their motto was "prevention is better than cure." This statement still holds much weight in the medical community today.

She was given the post of Professor of Gynaecology at the London School of Medicine for Women in 1875 and continued to express her beliefs for the remainder of her passionate career. By the year before her death, nearly 500 women were registered as doctors. Elizabeth deserves much recognition for her part in this amazing achievement and social change.

IN FOCUS
Women in Medicine

The modern world of medicine is far more welcoming to women than it has ever been, yet woman have been involved in health care since ancient times. Here we celebrate the achievements of women past and present.

Women have always held medical knowledge and been involved in the care of others, especially midwifery. Over the last few hundred years, many brave women have fought vehemently to be taken seriously in their medical careers. They rallied against established institutions that actively forbade or discouraged women from entering the arena of medicine, until their voices became too loud to ignore.

AGNODICE
(PAGE 8)

In ancient times, some women, such as Merit Ptah—the royal physician to the pharaoh of Egypt—did hold important positions. Despite being at a disadvantage, women have made great contributions to the understanding of health throughout history.

In ancient Greece, for example, Agnodice took great risks to become a doctor, disguising herself as a man in order to learn. Once her efficiency was recognized, rules were changed and women were allowed to be treated by female doctors.

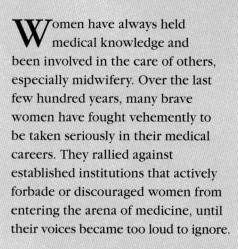

MARIA DALLE DONNE (PAGE 30)

As well as changing the face of health care, female scientists such as Tu Youyou and Alice Augusta Ball have also contributed greatly to the world of medicine via the invention of lifesaving drugs for malaria and leprosy.

TU YOUYOU (PAGE 100)

In the 1800s things began moving more quickly. Maria Dalle Donne was the first woman to receive a doctorate in medicine. She wrote extensively on the topic of female reproductive health and midwifery, and showed the world how talented female physicians could be—and how needed they were for the wellbeing of the patients.

Health awareness changed dramatically with the advent of large-scale war, especially during the Crimean War. Florence Nightingale changed the face of nursing and developed an approach to health care that tried to prevent disease through proper hygiene over searching for cures. Cleanliness was shockingly undervalued until she began promoting it in wartime hospitals. Not only did Florence increase public health standards as a result of her wartime nursing, her career made her job role far more respectable for women.

Many women stand at the forefront of medicine today; their vision and commitment to a happier and healthier population driving them toward improved medical systems. Their example, and the experiences of those equally remarkable women who preceeded them, will encourage and inspire each new generation of trailblazers who enter into the ever-expanding field of medicine.

ELIZABETH GARRETT ANDERSON
DOCTOR

1836–1917

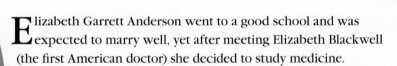

Elizabeth Garrett Anderson went to a good school and was expected to marry well, yet after meeting Elizabeth Blackwell (the first American doctor) she decided to study medicine.

Like Blackwell, she was met with resistance. After Elizabeth passed her exams at the Society of Apothecaries they changed the rules so that other women couldn't follow in her path.

In 1870 she became a visiting physician at the East London Hospital. After marrying, she learned French so she could gain a medical degree at the University of Paris. Sadly, her qualification wasn't recognized in Britain. Elizabeth refused to give in to prejudice, and eventually in 1876, laws were changed so that women could become medical professionals.

MARGARET HUGGINS
Astrophysicist

1848–1915

Margaret and her husband William are often described as the founders of astrophysics, the branch of science that applies the laws of physics to the study of stars and celestial bodies.

Together they contributed greatly to the world of astronomy yet it is only recently that Margaret's own input has been recognized. She downplayed how involved she was in order to promote William's public image—and avoid criticism for being a woman in science.

Yet Margaret was a talented astronomer with a keen interest in photography and spectroscopy. She even made her own spectroscope.

SOFIA KOVALEVSKAYA
MATHEMATICIAN

1850–1891

Sofia was the first Russian female mathematician to gain a doctorate from a European university. At an early age she studied mathematics, inspired by the walls of her room which were covered with papers from her father's days as a student.

Sofia's gender made it difficult for her to further her education in Russia—yet she persevered, marrying so that she could travel and moving to Berlin. Here she studied mathematics, wrote papers, and was eventually awarded her doctorate.

In 1880 she began teaching at the University of Stockholm, and six years later she was awarded a professorship. Her strong spirit and will to continue led to her acceptance.

HERTHA AYRTON
Inventor

1854–1923

Hertha became a respected scientist and inventor at a time when women were fighting to be a part of the academic world. Her early years were spent at her aunt's school, where she learned French, music, Latin, and mathematics. While working as a governess, she attended women's suffrage meetings where she met her mentor, Barbara Leigh Smith Bodicon, co-founder of Girton College, Cambridge. Hertha so impressed Bodicon that she was admitted to read mathematics.

Hertha then entered the world of science. She was the first woman to be a member of the Institution of Electrical Engineers, and registered more than 20 patents. One of her most significant inventions was a fan that could remove toxic gases, used in World War I to disperse mustard gas.

FLORENCE BASCOM

GEOLOGIST

1862–1945

CRYSTALLINE ROCK

Florence Bascom was a highly successful American geologist—the first woman to receive a PhD from John Hopkins University and the second to receive one for geology in the US.

She was also the first woman to be employed by the USGS (the United States Geological Survey) and her revolutionary influence can be seen in the great number of other women that entered into the world of earth sciences, following in her path.

Her early years were influenced by forward-thinking parents, who encouraged her to study at a time when it was very difficult for women to enter further education. Indeed, during her PhD, where she examined the formation of the Appalachian Mountain range, Florence had to sit behind a screen in case she distracted her male fellow students.

Florence carved a name for herself regardless, and she became widely known for her mapping of the rock formations in the states of Pennsylvania, Maryland, and New Jersey in the United States. She also utilized a relatively new field of geology—analyzing thin sections of rock using microscopes and light. Florence's passion can be seen in her own accounts of her work. For example, she described the fascination of her search for truth as coming from the pursuit of study itself, "where all the powers of the mind are absorbed in the task. One feels oneself in contact with something that is infinite and one finds a joy that is beyond expression in 'sounding the abyss of science' and the secrets of the infinite mind."

"I have considerable pride in the fact that some of the best work done in geology today by women, ranking with that done by men, has been done by my students."

She went on to have a successful career and, in 1894, was elected to the Geological Society of America. In 1906, she was named as one of the top 100 leading geologists in the very first issue of *American Men of Science*, and was the first woman to be elected to the Council of the Geological Society of America in 1924.

Florence also founded the geology department at Bryn Mawr College—the first in the US to offer an education to PhD level for women. She taught there for more than 30 years and was actively involved in ongoing research. As well as writing prolifically on her topic, an asteroid, a lake, and a crater have all been named after her, in recognition of her incredible work.

THIN SLICES OF ROCK STUDIED BY MICROSCOPE

ROCK SAMPLES

ANNIE JUMP CANNON
Astronomer

(1863–1941)

Annie Jump Cannon, nicknamed the "census-taker of the sky," was an amazing scientist in the field of astronomy, and is one of the leading female astronomers of all time. She was also an outspoken advocate of women's rights.

Her love of astronomy was initially inspired by her mother's love of the night sky, and as a child she would watch the stars from her attic. She later studied physics and astronomy at college in the US, at a time when it was still difficult for women to get ahead in the world of science.

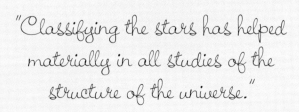

"Classifying the stars has helped materially in all studies of the structure of the universe."

MAGNIFYING LOUPE

She was extremely driven to achieve, stating that "I am sometimes very dissatisfied with life here. I do want to accomplish something so badly."

Annie became an assistant at the Harvard Observatory in 1896 after her mother's death, studying under Edward C. Pickering—the director at the time.

With Pickering, she worked to record and classify stars for the Henry Draper Catalog of Stellar Spectra in a team of talented female assistants. The current system was incredibly complex, so Annie eventually developed her own classification method using letters of the alphabet.

Annie based her system on star temperatures and this new approach of stellar spectra classification impressed many astronomers. It was universally adopted in 1922 and it is still in use today.

Amazingly, Annie classified more than 300,000 stars, discovering around 300 herself. In recognition of her vast contribution, she was awarded an honorary doctorate from the University of Oxford, England, in 1925. No other woman had been granted this award.

Annie became the curator of astronomical photographs for Harvard Observatory in 1911 and in 1938 was given the official title of Astronomer at Harvard, yet another first for a woman in her field.

Her amazing career is rightfully remembered for her dedication to her love of astronomy and her support of fellow women scientists, reportedly commenting that "it is hard to conceive of the time when mathematical or other scientific study by girls was so shocking to the conceptions of mankind that she must need do all her study secretly at night with a candle by her bedside."

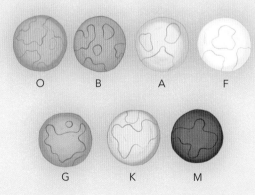

O   B   A   F

G   K   M

UNIVERSAL STAR CLASSIFICATIONS
DEVELOPED BY ANNIE JUMP CANNON

YNES ENRIQUETTA JULIETTA MEXIA

BOTANIST

1870–1938

Ynes Enriquetta Julietta Mexia was an American botanical collector—and explorer! At the age of 51, she joined the University of California and studied botany. She had worked as a social worker for many years beforehand. Ynes was so enthralled by her subject that she undertook a series of expeditions to collect plant specimens. She went to Mexico for two years, and was hired to go to Alaska as well. Amazingly, she also adventured through the Amazon River in South America, covering huge distances by canoe. Over 13 years, Ynes collected around 150,000 plant specimens, 500 of which were new species. Fifty of these are named after her.

MEXIANTHIS MEXICANUS

MAUD LEONORA MENTEN

BIOCHEMIST

1879–1960

NERVE CELL

Maud Menten was a Canadian pioneer in the world of scientific research, trailblazing the way for other female scientists.

She completed her medical degree in 1907 at the University of Toronto, then moved to New York to work in scientific research at the Rockefeller Institute. Maud is perhaps best known for her collaboration with Leonor Michaelis—their work led to the formulation of the Michaelis-Menten equation, which explained how enzymes behave. She went on to study cancer, earned a PhD in biochemistry, and professor of pathology at the University of Pittsburgh in 1918. She was conducted into the Canadian Medical Hall of Fame in 1998 for her enduring work.

RUTH MOUFANG
MATHEMATICIAN

1905–1977

Ruth Moufang, a German mathematician and daughter of a chemist, made ground-breaking contributions to the fields of geometry, yet during her career was denied permission to teach by the Nazi Minister of Education—simply because she was a woman.

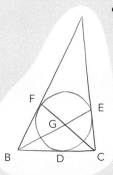

She studied at the University of Frankfurt, and was awarded her PhD in 1931 on projective geometry, a branch of mathematics concerned with questions of shape, size and properties of space. She spent a year researching in Rome before returning to Germany to give lectures on her topic, yet was unable to complete her teaching qualification to become a professor. Instead, she worked in a research institution, concentrating on elasticity theory—the first woman with a doctorate to do so. Finally, after the war in 1946 she was able to teach at the University of Frankfurt, and did so until she retired.

Ruth published several papers on mathematical theory leading to the development of the "Moufang theory," an equation that built on and improved the ideas of previous geometrists.

"A large part of her work is dedicated to the foundations of geometry. Her most outstanding contribution to this field is a result which adds a third important discovery to two others made previously by Hilbert."

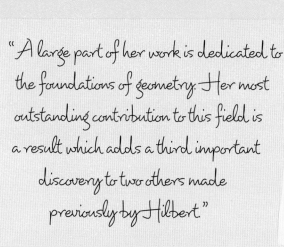

MARIA GOEPPERT MAYER

Physicist

1906–1972

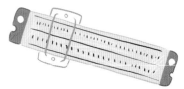

Maria Goeppert Mayer, a theoretical physicist, was born at the beginning of the twentieth century in Germany to a long line of intellectuals. Her father was a professor of paediatrics at Göttingen University, and Maria grew up there, spending much of her life around excellent teachers. She was awarded the Nobel Prize in 1963 with J. Hans D. Jensen for their joint work on the shell nuclear model (a model of the atomic nucleus concerning its energy levels).

"This was wonderful I liked the mathematics in it ... Mathematics began to seem too much like puzzle solving ... Physics is puzzle solving too, but of puzzles created by nature, not by the mind of man ... Physics was the challenge."

including Max Born, who was co-awarded the Nobel Prize in 1954 for his research in quantum mechanics, a theory concerned with atoms and subatomic particles. Her teachers quickly noticed her aptitude for learning and her talents.

In 1930, she married Joseph Mayer, and together they moved to Baltimore in the United States to work at the John Hopkins University. Maria wasn't appointed a position, unlike her husband, yet she continued working and making great advancements in the understanding of the benzene molecule.

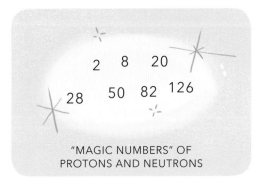

NOBEL PRIZE

In 1924 Maria began her own studies at Göttingen University, where she studied mathematics, which was still quite remarkable for a woman. She went on to do a PhD in physics under the guidance of three Nobel Prize winners,

2   8   20
28   50   82   126

"MAGIC NUMBERS" OF PROTONS AND NEUTRONS

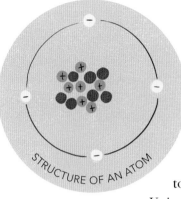

STRUCTURE OF AN ATOM

Husband and wife later moved to Columbia University in New York City in 1939. Here she was invited to join the Manhattan Project, and Maria worked on the chemical element uranium on a project involving the development of atomic bombs. After the war, in 1945, she volunteered as a professor of physics at the University of Chicago in the Enrico Fermi Institute for Nuclear Studies, eventually receiving a full appointment in 1959. She also taught at Sarah Lawrence College.

Throughout Maria's career she found it very difficult to find paid teaching work, yet this didn't put her off and she remained dedicated to her passion. She is best known for the development of the concept that a nucleus has many levels (shells), and that the stability of each nucleus depends on the positioning of protons and neutrons within the nucleus. She was rewarded with the Nobel Prize for her incredible work, reportedly saying that "winning the prize wasn't half as exciting as doing the work itself."

OLGA TAUSSKY-TODD
MATHEMATICIAN

1906–1995

Olga Taussky-Todd was a fantastic and prolific Jewish female mathematician. She wrote and published more than 300 papers across her career, and was awarded the Cross of Honour by Austria in recognition of her contribution to the world of mathematics.

She was born into a well-to-do Jewish family in 1906 in an area that is now part of the Czech Republic, yet moved to Austria as a young child. During World War I (1914–1918), her father began working as a director of a vinegar factory, and she was initially pressured to take over from him after his death. Her sister did so instead, which enabled Olga to study her true passion—mathematics—at the University of Vienna. Here, she attended meetings held by the Vienna Circle, a group of key thinkers who met to discuss and promote emerging philosophical ideas of the time.

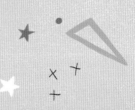

Olga attended the university, finishing her dissertation on number theory in 1930. She then held a one-year appointment at the Göttingen Mathematics Institute, where a fellow female mathematician warned her of the dangerous political situation arising in Germany. She later spent some time at both New York University and Bryn Mawr (the liberal women's college) in the US, and at Girton College, Cambridge, before settling in London.

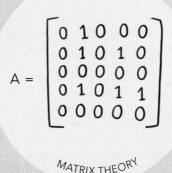

$$A = \begin{bmatrix} 0 & 1 & 0 & 0 & 0 \\ 0 & 1 & 0 & 1 & 0 \\ 0 & 0 & 0 & 0 & 0 \\ 0 & 1 & 0 & 1 & 1 \\ 0 & 0 & 0 & 0 & 0 \end{bmatrix}$$

MATRIX THEORY

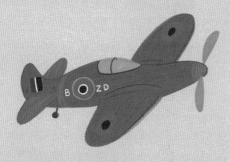

Here she married, and during World War II (1939–1945) worked at the National Physical Laboratory on aircraft design. The problems she worked on included ensuring the stability of planes.

This new vocation introduced her to matrix theory, which was important in the development of computers. In 1947, her husband, John Todd, received a placement at the National Bureau of Standards in Washington D.C. Olga continued writing paper on matrix theory and worked as a maths consultant there. Ten years later, they were invited to the California Institute of Technology to teach. Olga was appointed as a research associate, yet she taught and oversaw students through their theses. She was appointed a professor in 1971—an accolade that was long overdue.

Olga contributed much to the world of mathematics and supported other women in their pursuit of learning.

AUSTRIAN MEDAL FOR SCIENCE

"I felt that scientific experiments provided almost unlimited insight."

IN FOCUS
Women in Computing

Imagine a life without computers ... if you can? In the modern world it is hard to conceive of a day without using some form of computer technology—from our desktops to our washing machines and cars. Here we celebrate the women who have made our lives safer, easier, and more entertaining!

Computers have certainly made our lives infinitely easier and more efficient. They enable us to do so much, including travel far out into space and visit the depths of the oceans. We have many women to thank for their work in developing and advancing such important technology, for example, Ada Lovelace—one of the earliest pioneers, who came up with the original concept of writing computer programs.

It was during World War II, however, that women became far more involved in this relatively new technology. Women were needed to help the war effort, especially at Bletchley Park in the UK. Here many women, such as Joan Clarke, worked to break German codes, likely saving many millions of lives.

JOAN CLARKE (PAGE 84)

MARY KENNETH KELLER (PAGE 83)

Over the last 50 years there has been a steady increase in women being encouraged to study computing and other sciences. Most recently, STEM (science, technology, engineering, and mathematics) programs have been brought into education to ensure that topics such as computing are not monopolized by boys.

In the United States, Grace Hopper is well known for inventing COBOL—one of the first modern programming languages. Mary Kenneth Keller followed in her footsteps, developing another computer language known as BASIC, which opened up computing to the general public. She saw how relevant computers were for education, and believed that it was highly important for information to be available to everyone, so she dedicated her life to the mission of bringing computing to the masses.

The growth of NACA (the precursor to NASA) made further giant leaps in the advancement of computing technology, and women such as Mary Jackson were known as "human computers" for their expert work, making the necessary calculations that enabled the first US space flights.

CAROL SHAW (PAGE 114)

Women such as Carol Shaw, one of the first professional women working in video games, has shown there is a great place for women at the forefront of computing, and we need to ensure that future generations of girls continue to have the opportunity to show how inventive, intelligent, and forward-thinking they can be.

RACHEL CARSON
MARINE BIOLOGIST

1907–1964

Rachel Carson was a marine biologist and writer of the famous environmental book *Silent Spring*. This book revealed the harmful effects of pesticides and hugely influenced the general population's awareness of human impact on nature. It also contributed to the foundation of the Environmental Protection Agency (EPA).

zoology in 1932. She had to leave university to help support her family financially, yet she didn't give up on her passion for the environment.

In 1936, Rachel became the second woman ever to be hired by the US Bureau of Fisheries. Here, she was promoted to editor in chief, creating written content for the public as well as writing books such as *The Sea Around Us*. This book was translated into many different languages and became a national bestseller. Rachel believed it was important for people to love nature in order for them to be willing to do what it took to protect it, so her words were laced with a sense of curiosity and wonder to engage her readers with information.

BALD EAGLE

Born in 1907, Rachel showed a talent for writing from a very young age, contributing to children's magazines as a child. Her love of nature shone through throughout her education, and she was awarded a master's degree in

HER TYPEWRITER

She also began investigating the use of pesticides, and used a clever narrative in *Silent Spring* to appeal (and shock) its readers. Her message was clear: humans should not damage nature in order to progress technologically.

One of the main pesticides that Rachel wrote about was called DDT. Used as a bug-killer across the United States, it had originally been used in powder form to remove lice from soldiers in World War II. The wider effect of this substance on bird and plant life was incredibly damaging, and Rachel focused on how harmful it was.

"One way to open your eyes is to ask yourself, what if I had never seen this before? What if I knew I would never see it again?"

While Rachel was criticized by large chemical companies, she was also highly praised by others for having ideas ahead of her time. She called for new policies to protect human health as well as the environment, and her legacy has inspired generations of nature lovers to protect planet Earth.

MARY G. ROSS
Engineer and mathematician

1908–2008

Mary G. Ross was a true trailblazer. A well known engineer and mathematician, she is remembered for her important role in developing the technology which resulted in the launch of the American space program.

Mary was the great-granddaughter of Cherokee chief, John Ross, who had opposed the removal of his people from their native lands. She grew up in Tahlequah, the new settlement where the Cherokees were forced to move to from their homeland, before completing a degree in mathematics.

After her studies, she became a teacher and civil servant for the US Bureau of Indian Affairs before going back to university to complete a master's degree.

Then, during World War II, she was hired by the American aerospace company Lockheed as a mathematician. Her role was to research the effect of atmospheric pressure on military fighter planes. After the war, she continued to work for the company, who encouraged her to become qualified in engineering. Mary was highly interested in interplanetary spaceflight and soon began working on classified projects, including designs for craft involved in space missions.

Mary was an advocate for female engineers, and showed the world that women were just as capable of designing rockets and missiles as men!

"Math was more fun than anything else. It was always a game to me."

THE AGENA ROCKET

VIRGINIA APGAR
Medical doctor

1909–1974

Virginia Apgar made an amazing contribution to science; she developed a test for newborns just after birth to assess their health, thus saving many little lives.

Born in New Jersey in the US, Virginia showed a great interest in science growing up, choosing to study medicine at university. After she graduated, she studied how to administer anesthetics to patients about to undergo surgery. After two years of training, she was appointed as a director of anesthesia at Columbia University. Virginia struggled to be taken seriously due to her gender, yet she persevered and was eventually awarded the title of professor. She was the first woman there to ever hold this role.

Virginia focused her work on anesthesia and childbirth. She noticed that, just after a baby was born, doctors attended to the mother but paid little attention to the baby, which meant that potential problems were missed. Virginia saw a need for a new process to assess the health of the babies, creating a five-part test which looked at heart rate, breathing, muscle, reflexes, and skin tone. The system was used all over the world, to great effect.

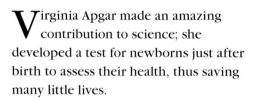

Virginia went on to discover which painkillers were harmful in childbirth and spent the rest of her career focusing on the care of newborns.

"Nine months' observation of the mother surely warrants one minute's observation of the baby."

MARGUERITE CATHERINE PEREY

CHEMIST

1909–1975

Marguerite Perey worked in the field of nuclear chemistry, and was a student of Marie Curie. She went on to discover the chemical element francium, the last element to be found outside of artificial laboratory settings.

After Marie Curie's death, which was caused by her exposure to radiation, Marguerite continued working on the element and was promoted to the role of radiochemist.

RADIOACTIVE
ATOM

Born in 1909 near Paris, France, Marguerite received a diploma in chemistry from Paris's Technical School of Women's Education in 1929. She then interviewed to work for Marie Curie, one of the most famous scientists of the day, aged just 19. What a first interview!

Amazingly, she got the job and began working at the Radium Institute, one of the world's leading physics and chemistry labs. Here, she learned how to work with radioactive elements. Her role was to prepare samples of the radioactive chemical element actinium, which had been discovered at the institute.

Then in 1935, Marguerite began examining a claim by other researchers, who believed that actinium emitted beta particles (fast-moving electrons). She believed that actinium was actually decaying into a completely different atom and through examination revealed this to be the case. This new element was named francium, after Marguerite's country of birth—France.

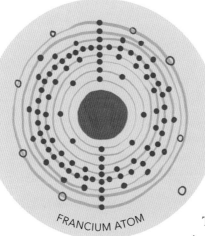

FRANCIUM ATOM

Francium is a very rare element, and it is estimated that only a few grams ever exist at any one time on Earth. Previous chemists had predicted its existence, yet to actually find it was extraordinary.

This incredible discovery raised Marguerite's profile in the world of science, and she was encouraged to study for a PhD. Rather fussily, she was initially denied because she didn't have an undergraduate degree. She had to study for the equivalent qualifications despite her clearly remarkable aptitude.

FRANCIUM

Once her PhD was eventually secured, Marguerite was awarded a senior position at the Radium Institute, and in 1949, became Chair of Nuclear Chemistry at the University of Strasbourg. Throughout the rest of her career she received many different awards, and was the first woman to join the French Academy of Sciences.

"It is my great hope that francium will be useful for the establishment of an early diagnosis of cancer. My unconditional wish would be to accomplish this task someday."

Marguerite passed away in 1975 from bone cancer, which was probably caused by working in close proximity with radiation for many years. Her life was truly inspirational—rising from a lowly lab technician to a star chemist.

BEATRICE SHILLING
Engineer

1909–1990

British Beatrice Shilling was a gifted aeronautical engineer—and racing driver! From a young age she had a fascination with machines, reportedly getting her first motorcycle at just 14. After school she worked as an electrician until she went to the University of Manchester, graduating with a master's degree in mechanical engineering.

Jobs were few and far between, yet she found work as a research assistant in the University of Birmingham until the Royal Air Force took her into employment at the Royal Aircraft Establishment.

It was during World War II that Beatrice made her greatest contribution to science. She found a solution to a very serious problem in the engines of fighter planes.

Imagine flying a Spitfire in the middle of an intense battle … you go into a nose dive to chase an enemy plane, yet the engine stalls … the carburettor is flooded with fuel. It's impossible to save the plane so you have to bail out with your parachute …

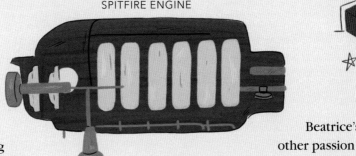

This was a reality for some pilots during the Battle of France and the Battle of Britain. Beatrice came to the rescue, however, and created a piece of equipment which could prevent the plane's fuel from

Beatrice's other passion was for motorbikes. She and her husband had a workshop at home, and enjoyed racing. She was even given an award for completing a racetrack at over 100 miles an hour. It has been said that she refused to marry her husband until he too received the award!

Beatrice continued to work for the Royal Aircraft Establishment after the war in the Mechanical Engineering Department and was a member of the Women's Engineering Society. She worked on numerous projects throughout her career showing that the world of engineering was for women as well as men.

THE "TILLY ORIFICE"

flooding the engine. This small brass object was affectionately nicknamed the "Tilly orifice" by pilots. The invention saved many lives, and made it possible for Allied pilots to successfully attack German planes.

TOOLS FOR MAKING MACHINE PARTS

"Her idea of relaxation was to drive a car at full throttle, and if the car wasn't fast enough, her workbench was there in the back room to machine new parts to make it faster."

MATTHEW FREUDENBERG

JOY ADAMSON

Naturalist

1910–1980

Joy Adamson is best known for her love of African wildlife and the promotion of its care and protection. She was an artist, writer, and naturalist, and is credited with raising awareness on the need to protect and nurture the environment.

Joy grew up in Austria-Hungary in a wealthy family. While married to her first husband, she moved to Africa and fell in love with the continent. She also met the man who would become her second husband and decided to stay, painting African plants and creating portraits of indigenous people.

Joy's third husband was a game warden called George Adamson.

LEOPARD FAMILY

One day, George came to Joy and told her that sadly he had had to shoot a lion to defend himself, and had discovered that it had cubs. They decided to keep one—Elsa—and Joy became very close to her. Eventually, they released Elsa back into the wild, and were able to follow her progress as she had three cubs.

In 1960, Joy published *Born Free*, which gave an account of her time with the lion, as well as establishing the Elsa Wild Animal Appeal. The book was made into a highly popular film. In later life Joy worked with other animals, including leopards and cheetahs.

She was tragically killed, yet her legacy lives on—we remember her for her amazing capability to bond with animals and show they need our protection.

"As I watched this beautiful pair (of lions), I realized how all the characteristics of our cubs were inherent in them. Indeed, in every lion I saw during our searches I recognized the intrinsic nature of Elsa, Jespah, Gopa, and Little Elsa, the spirit of all the magnificent lions in Africa."

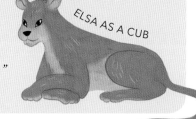

ELSA AS A CUB

DOROTHY CROWFOOT HODGKIN

CHEMIST

1910–1994

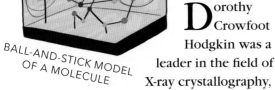

BALL-AND-STICK MODEL OF A MOLECULE

Dorothy Crowfoot Hodgkin was a leader in the field of X-ray crystallography, a powerful method for finding out the particle arrangements of crystals. She won the Nobel Prize for chemistry for her determination of the structures of molecules of vitamin B12. She also developed the methods that made these discoveries possible. Dorothy showed a keen interest in crystals from a young age, and studied chemistry at the University of Oxford as an undergraduate. She then attended the University of Cambridge, where she worked in the lab of John Desmond Bernal, a physicist who encouraged her

passion. In 1934, she helped take the first X-rays of the digestive enzyme pepsin. Dorothy then returned to Oxford, where she taught at Somerville college (for women). Margaret Thatcher, British prime minister from 1979–1990, was one of her pupils.

"I was captured for life by chemistry and by crystals."

During World War II, Dorothy studied penicillin, a group of antibiotics, as there was a great demand for this medicine, and she later examined the structure of different vitamins as well as the hormone insulin for over 30 years.

Dorothy's contributions to science were widely celebrated and recognized. Without her passion, talent and skills, our understanding of molecules would be far lesser— she truly made the world a more enlightened place.

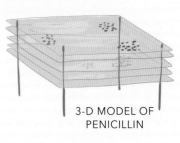

3-D MODEL OF PENICILLIN

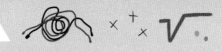

DOROTHY JOHNSON VAUGHAN
MATHEMATICAL ENGINEER

1910–2008

Dorothy Johnson Vaughan was an African-American mathematics teacher who became a leader in the field of mathematical engineering during the early development of aerospace technology. Her legacy is remarkable.

Born in Missouri, Dorothy taught at a school in Virginia after finishing university. She married and started working for the National Advisory Committee for Aeronautics (NACA), which NASA later took over from. During the 1940s there was a great need for engineers and mathematicians to develop aircraft technology due to World War II. As so many men were needed to serve and fight, more women were hired and their genius and capability was revealed.

Dorothy began her working life at a time when racial discrimination was being reformed, yet she was still made to work separately from her white colleagues— segregation was still, awfully, commonplace.

At NACA, Dorothy rose through the ranks and became a successful manager of the West Area Computing programming. She was the organisation's first black supervisor and worked tirelessly to increase opportunities for women. When NASA took over from NACA, she then joined the new Analysis and Computation Division, where thankfully segregation was at last removed. Here, Dorothy developed her programming skills to expert level. She taught herself FORTRAN, the general purpose programming language used in scientific computing. She also

ALPHA KAPPA ALPHA SORORITY

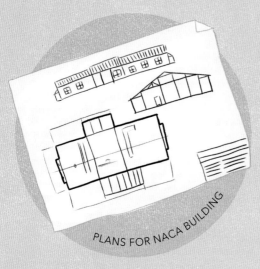

PLANS FOR NACA BUILDING

contributed greatly to the development of the Scout Launch Vehicle Program—one of NASA's most successful launch vehicles. Dorothy ensured that her female staff were highly trained in programming, foreseeing its future importance in the industry.

She is featured in the book *Hidden Figures: The Story of the African-American Women Who Helped Win the Space Race*, which was also made into a film in 2016.

"I changed what I could, and what I couldn't, I endured."

CALCULATING MACHINE

MARIE PARIS PIŞMIŞ DE RECILLAS
Astronomer

1911–1999

Marie Paris Pişmiş de Recillas was an inspirational astronomer—not only establishing the study of astronomy in Mexico, but also encouraging many other women to follow in her footsteps.

She was born in Istanbul in 1911 into a high society family, and attended an elite school, where she excelled at mathematics. Marie was one of the first women to graduate from her course at the Science School of Istanbul University—already she was making headway in a male-dominated world.

Marie then went on to teach

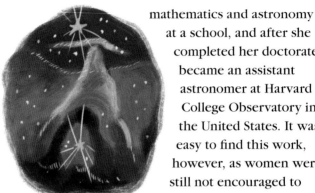

PISMIS 24

TRIANGULUM GALAXY

mathematics and astronomy at a school, and after she completed her doctorate, became an assistant astronomer at Harvard College Observatory in the United States. It wasn't easy to find this work, however, as women were still not encouraged to work in astronomy. It was here, however, that she met her future husband, Félix Recillas, and was able to develop her skills surrounded by a plethora of established astronomers.

Together Marie and Félix settled in Mexico (where he was from), and she became the first professional astronomer in the country, working at the Tonantzintla Observatory of Puebla and the National Observatory of Tacubaya. Marie worked here for more than 50 years and

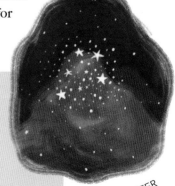

STAR CLUSTER

"She was an effective role model for young women. As a result, of the 80 astronomers currently at the Institute, a relatively high proportion (25 percent) are women."

SILVIA TORRES-PIEMBERT AT MARIE'S DEATH IN 1999

was highly celebrated for her contribution to the field, particularly her study of the structure of our galaxy and her interest in new techniques to study nebulae.

She wrote prolifically throughout her career, with more than 120 papers being published in highly respected journals. Her research was known to be excellent and more than 20 star clusters are named after her. Marie also edited several astronomical journals, as well as

SPIRAL GALAXY

writing the curriculum for studying astronomy at her observatory.

Marie was a true pioneer in the world of astronomy, devotedly promoting the science. She is a great example of a true leader in that she made other leaders— many of her students became well-known astronomers in their own right.

ASTRID LØKEN

Entomologist and Wartime Spy

1911–2008

Astrid Løken was the first female member of the Norwegian Entomological Society, an organization that promotes the study of insects. Astrid herself was primarily interested in bumblebees and this was her main scientific focus.

She was also, however, heavily involved in the resistance to the German occupation of Norway during World War II. Astrid joined the intelligence organization known as XU, and was given the anonymous name "Eva" to operate under. During her undercover work, she took photographs of both insects—and the geography of the land, developing the images in secret and collating information under the cover of darkness. Remarkably, Astrid carried a cyanide pill with her at all times in case she was caught by the enemy. She even reportedly had hand grenades in her bedroom!

> "I was never scared if I came alive or dead out of it, [the research] was too important."

After the war, Astrid spent a short time in the US before returning to Norway and her work in science. She was employed at both the Norwegian College of Agriculture and the Bergen Museum where she built up their insect collection. She retired in the late 1970s, yet moved to the University of Oslo to work as a research fellow for another decade.

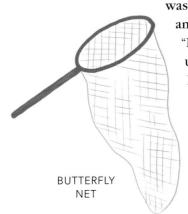

BUTTERFLY NET

BUMBLEBEE

MARY KENNETH KELLER
COMPUTER SCIENTIST

1913–1985

Mary Kenneth Keller is known for being the first woman in the United States to be awarded a degree in computer science. She was also, perhaps surprisingly, a nun!

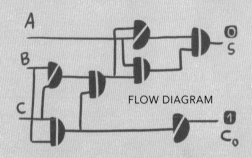

FLOW DIAGRAM

Mary was born in Ohio, and at the age of eighteen she entered the religious institute Sisters of Charity of the Blessed Virgin Mary. She took her vows and also studied mathematics at a bachelor degree level, and mathematics and physics at a master's level. She then earned her PhD—a huge step forward for women in the field of science.

Mary went on to work at a male-only computer science institute

111011
00111101000
000110111110
101010 1111100
0011111 00 11110
110111

COMPUTER CODE

at Dartmouth College, and it was here that she helped develop a computer language known as BASIC. This new method of writing computer code was revolutionary—now anyone could learn to program. Her contribution made computing for more available to the general public. She was interested in artificial intelligence many decades ago, stating that: "For the first time, we can now mechanically simulate the cognitive process. We can make studies in artificial intelligence."

"We're having an information explosion, and it's certainly obvious that information is of no use unless it's available."

ĽUDMILA PAJDUŠÁKOVÁ
Astronomer

1916–1979

L'udmila is best known for finding not one, but five comets! After leaving her job as a teacher, she began working at Skalnate Pleso Observatory in the Tatra mountains in Slovakia, where she later became director in the late 1950s. L'udmila completed her studies in astronomy at Bratislava University, and then set to work photographing meteors and searching the sky for comets. She also specialized in studying and observing the Sun's corona (the outermost parts of its atmosphere). A member of the International Astronomy Union, L'udmila is a great inspiration to women who want to follow their passion.

COMET

ENIGMA MACHINE

JOAN CLARKE
Mathematician

1917–1996

Joan Clarke is remembered for being the only woman in the circle of codebreakers that cracked the German Enigma machine during World War II at Bletchley Park, UK. Joan was recruited after graduating from Cambridge University with a degree in mathematics, though she wasn't given the full award as women weren't able to receive a full degree until 1948. After joining Bletchley Park, Joan's talent was noticed, and she was promoted to the role of linguist—despite speaking no other languages—to allow her to receive a pay rise. She worked alongside Alan Turing, developing the system to decode the secret messages sent by the Nazis using their Enigma machine. In doing so, they changed the course of the war.

GERTRUDE B. ELION
PHARMACOLOGIST

1918–1999

Gertrude B. Elion was an American pharmacologist famous for receiving a shared Nobel Prize for her discovery of medicines to treat gout, malaria, herpes, and leukemia, as well as drugs used to prevent patients' bodies rejecting kidney transplants.

She grew up in New York, and graduated from university with a degree in chemistry in the late 1930s. Gertrude then worked as a lab assistant, a food analyst, and a high school teacher before completing a master's degree, also in chemistry.

During World War II, she started work at the company now known as GlaxoSmithKline. Here she developed such a vast array of life-saving drugs, alongside George H. Hitchings. She later became a head of department and continued to work at the lab after retirement, developing the drug treatment for AIDS.

KATHERINE G. JOHNSON
MATHEMATICIAN

1918–

APOLLO 11

Katherine G. Johnson, a talented mathematician, worked for the US space program during the early days of space flight, and enjoyed a long career in the field. She was also one of a select group of African-American women working for NASA at the time, overcoming racial prejudice during a time of segregation.

Katherine always had a way with numbers, starting high school three years early, when she was just 10 years old. She went on to receive degrees in both mathematics and French. She was later chosen by NASA because of her expert problem-solving skills. Katherine made all kinds of important calculations for space flight, including the safe return of the Apollo astronauts from the moon.

KATERYNA YUSHCHENKO
COMPUTER SCIENTIST AND MATHEMATICIAN

1919–2001

Kateryna Yushchenko developed one of the most important computer languages, revolutionizing the way we use technology today, despite a difficult start to her university education.

In 1937, when Kateryna was studying physics and mathematics at Kyiv University, her father was arrested for supposedly being a Ukrainian nationalist. This led to her expulsion by association. Kateryna's mother took papers to demonstrate her husband's innocence, yet the secret police burned them, and she too was locked away.

After World War II, Kateryna worked with an academic, Boris Vladimirovich Gnedenko, securing her PhD in 1950. Kateryna later moved to Kiev with him to work at the Institute of Mathematics of the Ukrainian Academy of Sciences.

In the 1950s, the MESM computer was transferred to the Institute, and Kateryna was one of the people to operate it. This was the first universally programmable computer in the Soviet Union—yet Kateryna improved it by creating a new programming language. Over her career, she created a school of programming—an incredible achievement and one that has had enormous ripple effects on the modern world.

STATE PRIZE OF THE UKRAINIAN SSR MEDAL

MAINFRAME COMPUTER

SHE NEVER FORGOT HER HOMETOWN, AS SHE WROTE IN THIS POEM CALLED *MY CITY*:

I'll never forget you, I'll come there once more,
As soon as we crash the spine of our evil foe.
I hope, my dear city, that you understand,
I'll meet you again, when I'm back, in the end.

MARY JACKSON
Mathematician

1921–2005

Mary Jackson worked as a research mathematician at NACA (the precursor to NASA) and was one of the "human computers" that worked in its West Area Computing Unit within a team of highly talented African-American women. Here, she made calculations for the first American space missions.

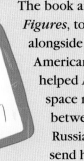

The book and film, *Hidden Figures*, told her story, alongside two other African-American women who helped America in the space race (the race between the US and Russia to successfully send humans into space).

Mary was working at a time of extreme racial segregation—at NACA there were separate eating areas and bathrooms for black people and white people. Despite such awful, unequal treatment, Mary was promoted to aeronautical engineer in 1958 at NASA; their first black female engineer. Her knowledge and intellect was invaluable in the development of aircraft flight, and her inspirational career spanned more than three decades. Later in life she worked to ensure equal opportunities within the space organization, promoting the role of women throughout NASA.

"I plan on being an engineer at NASA. But I can't do that without taking those classes at that all-white high school. And I can't change the color of my skin. So, I have no choice … but to be the first."

THE PRESIDENTIAL MEDAL OF FREEDOM

KATHLEEN ANTONELLI
MATHEMATICIAN AND COMPUTER SCIENTIST

1921–2006

Kathleen McNulty Mauchly Antonelli had a tough start in life. On the day of her birth her father was arrested and sent to prison—he was an officer in the IRA during the Irish War of Independence. On his release, the family left County Donegal and emigrated to Philadelphia, in the US.

TRANSISTOR

Kathleen developed her affinity for mathematics at an early age. After high school she enrolled at the Chestnut Hill College for Women. During her third year, Kathleen found out that she would most likely only get a career in teaching. In order to avoid that career path, Kathleen studied accounting, business law, economics, and more, so that she would be extra employable. In 1942, out of a class of ninety-two, she was one of only a few who graduated with a degree in mathematics.

During World War II Kathleen got a job with the army to calculate bullet and missile paths. Stationed at the Ballistic Research Laboratory at the Aberdeen Proving Ground in Maryland, her job title was "Human Computer." Computing ballistics' paths used for artillery firing tables was done using basic calculators and large sheets of paper. Each firing

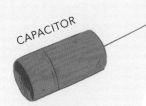
CAPACITOR

table had about 1,800 paths. Computing just one path took 30–40 hours of work.

After a couple of months, Kathleen was transferred to the Moore School of Engineering to work on the Differential Analyzer; the largest and most sophisticated calculator of the time. There were only six in the world. This machine compacted 40 hours of work into approximately 50 minutes. Kathleen was promoted to supervise these calculations.

"All the years I gave talks about the ENIAC (Electronic Numerical Integrator and Computer), I always talked about it as John [Mauchly, her first husband]'s story, not my story."

VACUUM TUBES

Kathleen was selected to be one of the first programmers on the ENIAC (Electronic Numerical Integrator and Computer), developed between 1943 and 1946. It could complete the same calculations as the Differential Analyzer in less than 20 seconds. Working only from blueprints of the machine, her responsibility was to determine the sequence of steps required to complete the calculations for each problem. Kathleen subsequently invented the subroutine, meaning that they would no longer have to repeat a whole program. Despite being given no praise for their work on the world's first general-purpose computer at the time, Kathleen and the other programmers were inducted into the Women in Technology International Hall of Fame in 1997.

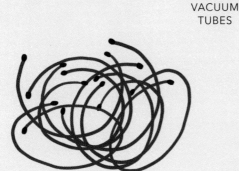
COMPUTER CABLES

EUGENIE CLARK

Marine Biologist

1922–2015

Eugenie Clark is affectionately nicknamed "the shark lady" due to her love of sharks. During her childhood she spent many weekends at her local aquarium in New York, and she grew to love the ocean and its creatures.

Eugenie learned to dive, and became an ichthyologist (a fish biologist). She studied how sharks behave and spent a lot of time on expeditions. She ventured to the Red Sea in Egypt,

GENIE'S DOGFISH, *SQUALUS CLARKAE*

"When you see a shark underwater, you should say 'How lucky I am to see this beautiful animal in his environment.'"

writing a book—*Lady with a Spear*—about her underwater experiences there.

Eugenie then worked at a small laboratory in Florida, in the US, where she studied and taught widely about sharks. Amazingly, she dived all the way up until she was 92! Her work inspired marine conservation and her speeches helped show the public how fascinating and special sharks truly are.

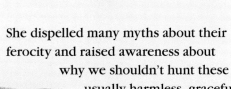

BASKING SHARK

She dispelled many myths about their ferocity and raised awareness about why we shouldn't hunt these usually harmless, graceful creatures. In 2018 a species of dogfish, a type of shark, was named after her.

SULAMITH GOLDHABER
PHYSICIST

1923–1965

Austrian-born Sulamith is best known for her pioneering work in the field of particle physics. She met her husband Gerson Goldhaber while they were studying in Jerusalem. Together, they moved to the University of Wisconsin, where they both studied physics and received PhDs.

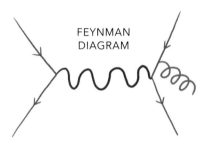

FEYNMAN DIAGRAM

They became experts in nuclear emulsion technology (technology used to detect charged particles), often using the Bevatron particle accelerator at Berkeley. This machine accelerated subatomic particles to high velocities, and was the most powerful machine of its kind at that time. Together they made important discoveries, presenting their findings to the world of science to great acclaim.

CMS COLLISION EVENTS

In the 1960s, Sulamith moved her area of study to the world of "bubble chambers," chambers filled with a hot liquid, such as hydrogen, to track

"Her talk (on heavy mesons and hyperons at the 1956 Rochester Conference) marked the turning point in the study of strange particles"

LUIS ALVAREZ

electrically charged particles. She soon became an expert, writing scientific papers, speaking at international events, and visiting places such as the CERN laboratory in Switzerland.

Very sadly she died in her early 40s, yet the world remembers Sulamith for her remarkable scientific skill and devotion to her passion.

STEPHANIE LOUISE KWOLEK

Chemist

1923–2014

Born in Pennsylvania in the US, Stephanie wanted to be a doctor when she grew up, and in 1946 she received a Bachelor of Science degree in chemistry from the Carnegie Mellon University. With her degree she took a temporary job at the chemical firm DuPont where she hoped to earn enough money to study medicine. However, medicine was not how Stephanie would go on to save lives.

Stephanie found her work at DuPont too interesting to leave. She was researching polymers, compounds with high molecular weight made by the addition of many smaller molecules. A few years later, she made her biggest discovery—Kevlar.

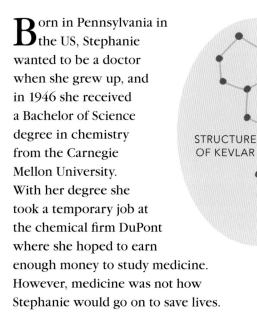

STRUCTURE OF KEVLAR

KEVLAR BULLETPROOF JACKET AND HELMET

In 1964, anticipating a fuel shortage, DuPont wanted to find a way to make vehicle wheels lighter, for better fuel economy. Kwolek's laboratory began searching for a new material. It was in a cloudy solution that would usually have been thrown away that Stephanie made the discovery. She persuaded her colleague to use the spinner to test her solution. They were amazed to find

"Not in a million years did I think the discovery of this liquid solution would save thousands of lives."

that this produced a thread that was stronger than Nylon. In futher tests, they found that it was five times stronger than steel of the same weight!

The laboratory director at DuPont understood the significance of this discovery, so they opened a new field of polymer chemistry. Through further research, Kwolek learned that the threads could be made even stronger through heating them, and she continued to research Kevlar derivatives until her retirement.

KEVLAR GLOVES

She went on to receive more acclaim for her discovery—she was inducted into the American National Inventors Hall of Fame and the National Women's Hall of Fame. The Royal Society of Chemistry in the UK has a Stephanie L. Kwolek Award that recognizes exceptional contributions to chemistry.

The results of her genius can be found in many things from mooring ropes to optical cables used for broadband and televisions, aircraft parts to bulletproof vests. Many, many lives have been saved, and injuries prevented, by the use of Kevlar in protective clothing.

For her discovery, Stephanie Kwolek was awarded the DuPont company's Lavoisier Medal for outstanding technical achievement. At the time of her death in 2014, she was the only female employee to receive that award.

KEVLAR THREAD

EVA KLEIN

BIOLOGIST

1925–

CELL

Eva Klein has made an incredible contribution to science and is partly responsible for raising Sweden to a such prominent position in successful cancer research.

Born in Hungry in 1925 to a Jewish family, Eva was discriminated against for her religion during the German occupation of her country. Indeed, during the last years of World War II, her medical studies were interrupted and she was forced into hiding.

After the war Eva finished her education and married George Klein, also a medical student. They moved to Sweden, where she finished her medical degree and she became an assistant professor at the Karolinska Institute, in 1948.

"Let us teach our children to use their own minds."

MOUSE

Eva concentrated her work on cell research and genetics, where she looked into how genes in normal cells can suppress cancer cells, and worked extensively on Burkitt's lymphoma.

She also wrote about "natural killer" cells (a type of white blood cell), which were discovered at the institute. This work paved the way for many other researchers in the field of immunology, cell biology, and cancer. She has been recognized by national academies in Sweden, Hungary, and the United States.

VERA RUBIN
Astronomer

1928–2016

DARK MATTER

Vera Rubin, an American astronomer, revealed to the world that much of the matter in the universe is dark. She was also a champion for other female scientists, proving to the world that women held just as much weight and intellect as men. It was not easy for her to advance in her career, yet her willingness to persevere despite discrimination is inspirational to us all.

Her main discovery was that stars that orbit around a spiral galaxy move at high speeds whether they are in the middle of the galaxy or on its edge. This was remarkable as it went against the accepted theories of gravity. From this observation, it was revealed that the mass of a galaxy extended beyond its most visible parts, such as stars. The name for this extra mass is dark matter.

Born in Pennsylvania, Vera was fascinated with the night sky from a young age, leading her to choose to study astronomy to PhD level. Her thesis showed that galaxies tend to sit together in clumps. Vera taught at Georgetown University, then moved to the Carnegie Institution's Department of Terrestrial Magnetism in Washington DC. Here she taught and mentored many generations of both male and female scientists, leading them onto great successes of their own.

"Worldwide, half of all brains are in women."

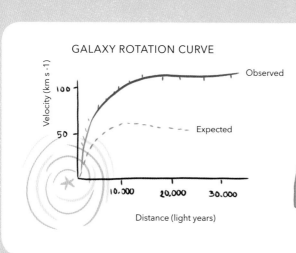

GALAXY ROTATION CURVE

Velocity (km s -1)

Observed

Expected

100

50

10,000   20,000   30,000

Distance (light years)

IN FOCUS
Women in Chemistry

Women have been involved in chemistry since the days of alchemy, but it has only been in the last few hundred years that they have been allowed to work in the field in a significant way—and their contributions have been invaluable.

Early female scientists had to fight to prove themselves and be taken seriously at an academic level. We must remember them, and thank them for paving the way for more women in science today.

Women such as Jane Marcet, credited as the first female science writer, made the basics of chemistry accessible via printed books. In the preface to her book *Conversations on Chemistry*, she stated that:

JANE
MARCET
(PAGE 26)

"In venturing to offer to the public, and more particularly to the female sex, an introduction to chemistry, the author, herself a woman, conceives that some explanation may be required; and she feels it the more necessary to apologize for the present undertaking, as her knowlege of the subject is but recent, and as she can have no real claims to the title of a chemist."

Despite the gender gap that Jane Marcet drew attention to, women continued to apply themselves to learning the mysteries of matter. They investigated the properties and reactions of different elements and saw how chemical reactions formed new substances.

worked closely with chemical elements. Indeed, Marie discovered both polonium (Po) and radium (Ra). Dorothy Crowfoot Hodgkin is another example of a woman creating revolutionary work in chemistry. She was a British chemist, who developed and advanced a technique used to determine 3-D structures of molecules. She was the third woman ever to receive the Nobel Prize in chemistry.

Many other women have made great contributions to the wonderful world of chemistry and this will continue into the future. We need girls to continue to enter the field and add their enthusiasm and vision to the study of matter!

ALICE AUGUSTA BALL (PAGE 52)

Indeed, women have made some of the most monumental and impactful studies in chemistry. Alice Augusta Ball, for example, developed the first successful treatment for the devastating disease leprosy. Gertrude B. Elion also helped discover medicines that could treat deadly diseases such as leukemia. These women have improved the health of many thousands of people, changing their lives for the better.

Marie Curie and her daughter Irène famously worked together in the mid-nineteenth century, and though often associated with physics, also

DOROTHY CROWFOOT HODGKIN (PAGE 77)

GLORIA LIM

MYCOLOGIST

1930–

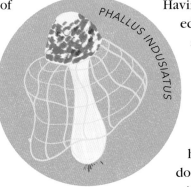

PHALLUS INDUSIATUS

Gloria Lim has had a lot of "firsts" in her life. She was awarded a first-class degree in botany for her studies at university. She went on to become the first woman to hold the position of Dean of the Faculty of Science at the University of Singapore, and then the first woman to head the Department of Botany at the National University of Singapore. After her retirement she became the first director of Singapore's National Institute of Education. All because of the amazing work and research she has done in the field of mycology—the study of fungi.

GANODERMA ELFVINGI

Having gained a diploma in education, Gloria taught at a girl's school while also teaching at the University of Malaya, where she received her master's degree. She went to London to get her PhD, and became a doctor of fungus. As if that wasn't enough, Gloria then received a Fulbright Fellowship (an American cultural exchange program with the goal of improving intercultural relations through the exchange of knowledge and skills) so she went to Berkeley in California. It was here that she went from botany to mycology, and soon became one of the world's leading experts on all things mushroom-related.

She was such an expert that the Singaporean Ministry of Defence hired her when their underground storage bunkers developed a fungal infection and they needed it removing.

"Yes, [fungi] can cause disease, but they can also heal you. Important drugs like penicillin were first found in fungi."

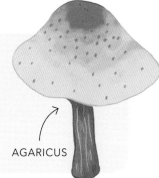

AGARICUS

SHIITAKE

Gloria was asked to work on the advisory board for a company who developed mushrooms for medicines, like penicillin. She has written hundreds of research papers, articles, and chapters in books on mycology, many of which are still being used as reference for new generations looking to follow in her footsteps and study fungal biology.

Through her studies Gloria had assembled an enormous collection of fungal species. When she retired, the botany and zoology departments merged, and the focus shifted to zoology. Her whole collection was destroyed, because fungi is generally considered "problematic."

Following her retirement from the world of mycology, Gloria dedicated her days to the National Institute of Education. As its very first director she has been instrumental in launching university programs of all levels. Now the future scientists of Singapore have somewhere at home to study and do their research. They don't have to travel abroad, as Gloria did, to follow their dreams.

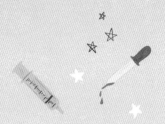

TU YOUYOU
Pharmacologist

1930–

Tu Youyou has made one of the most significant contributions to the world of medicine—she developed a drug that drastically improved survival rates for those suffering from the disease malaria. Over half of the world's population are at risk from malaria, so this was an incredible achievement.

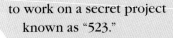

MALARIA MOSQUITO

Tu was born in China and went to Peking University School of Medicine to study pharmacology. She then studied Traditional Chinese Medicine. Her combined knowledge led to her being chosen to work on a secret project known as "523."

The task of curing malaria had been given to a select few, and Tu went to a remote island to witness its devastating effects.

Tu knew that in traditional chinese medicine, sweet wormwood was used to treat fevers, one of the main symptoms of malaria, which is spread by insects carrying a certain parasite. She discovered that a substance within the plant—artemisinin—stops the parasite. This led to drugs based on artemisinin being created, and in the last few decades, more than two hundred million malaria patients have been treated. She received the Nobel Prize for this incredible work.

ARTEMISIA ANNUA

"Drugs based on artemisinin have led to the survival and improved health of millions of people."

THE NOBEL PRIZE ORGANIZATION

DIAN FOSSEY
PRIMATOLOGIST AND CONSERVATIONIST

1935–1985

"When you realize the value of all life, you dwell less on what is past and concentrate on the preservation of the future."

conservation, dedicating her life to threatened gorillas.

Growing up in California in the US, Dian showed a keen interest in animals from a young age, especially horses. Her stepfather, who was reportedly emotionally distant from her, disapproved of her direction in life, leaving her with little financial assistance. After working as an occupational therapist, and living on a farm, she made the giant leap to Africa, self-funding her trip.

During this journey, her vision and dream was cemented. She explored the continent and met gorillas for the first time. On her return to the United States she learned the African language Swahili and prepared for a longer visit. During her time in Africa, she immersed herself in the observation of mountain gorillas, battling with a difficult political climate and limited help. She made friends with one gorilla in particular, called Digit. Dian wrote the book *Gorillas in the Mist*, detailing her experiences.

Dian Fossey is known for her passionate love for and study of mountain gorillas in the depths of the cloud forests of Rwanda, Africa. She was tragically killed, yet her life's work demonstrated how powerful one woman's love for animals could be—she poured her heart and soul into wildlife

SILVERBACK GORILLA

ELSA GUÐBJÖRG VILMUNDARDÓTTIR

GEOLOGIST

1932–2008

Elsa was Iceland's first female geologist, studying in both Reykjavik and Stockholm in Sweden. Her geological research has been of major assistance to Iceland's Electricity Department, working for both them and then the National Energy Authority of Iceland from the late 1960s till her retirement. Her tasks included supervising a project that involved geographical land mapping, as well as mapping landscapes affected by volcanic eruptions. Elsa wrote about her research and contributed to a book on the landscape of south Iceland.

RING VOLCANO

ETTA ZUBER FALCONER

MATHEMATICIAN

1933–2003

Etta is celebrated for being a highly talented and insightful mathematician, as well as a remarkable promoter of education specifically for African-Americans, being awarded the Louise Hays Award in recognition of her efforts. She was one of the first generation of African-American women to gain a PhD, and she dedicated almost four decades to teaching at the Spelman College Department of Mathematics, inspiring hundreds of students to learn and explore the beauty of numbers.

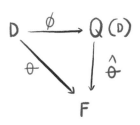

JOSEFINA CASTELLVÍ PIULACHS
Oceanographer

1935–

Josefina Castellví Piulachs is a highly respected oceanographer. She has written extensively on oceans and Antarctica. In 1953, she began studying biology at the University of Barcelona before receiving her PhD in oceanography in her mid-twenties. After she joined the Institute of Marine Sciences, she became the first Spaniard to join an international expedition to Antarctica. In 1987 she was part of a team that established the first Spanish base in Antarctica. She ran the base, which housed up to 12 scientists for four months of the year, while continuing her research into marine bacteria, earning a prestigious medal from the University of Barcelona. In retirement, Josefina continues to give lectures on the coldest place on Earth.

MEEMANN CHANG
Paleontologist

1936–

MEEMANNIA

Meemann Chang is a Chinese paleontologist (a scientist that studies fossils). She was the first woman to become the head of the Institute of Vertebrate Paleontology and Paleoanthropology and has had many extinct species named after her. These include the fish *Meemannia*, the dinosaur *Sinovenator changii* and the bird *Archaeornithura meemannae*. Through her study of fish fossils, she has found some of our earliest ancestors, and disproved the notion that lungfish were an evolutionary link between marine life and humans. In 2018 she was given the L'Oréal UNESCO For Women in Science Award in recognition of the significance of her work and career.

MARY ALLEN WILKES
Computer Programmer and Designer

1937–

Nowadays, most people have a smartphone, which acts like a mini computer that you can carry around. However, not so long ago smart phones didn't exist. Instead people had personal computers. One of the first of those now recognized as a personal computer was called LINC and it is for the work with the LINC computer that we now celebrate Mary Allen Wilkes.

Born in Chicago, Mary grew up wanting to be a lawyer. She studied philosophy and theology, planning to go on to law school. Unfortunately, she was discouraged from this path because of the challenge women faced in the world of law (it was very male dominated).

Mary remembered that her geography teacher had said that she "ought to be a computer programmer" and so she became one. She worked at the renowned Massachusetts Institute of Technology (MIT) on the Speech

PARTS OF THE LINC MACHINE

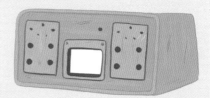

Recognition Project at Lincoln Laboratory. She then joined the Digital Computer Group as work was starting on LINC. Mary's contributions included simulating its operation during its design phase; designing the console for the prototype; and even writing the operating manual for the final console design.

Eventually the LINC group left Lincoln Laboratory to form the Center for Computer Technology at MIT's Cambridge campus. It was there that Mary taught the participants how to use the LINC Assembly Program and co-authored the LINC's programming manual.

Mary left the LINC group to travel the world for a year, but she rejoined the group on her return, living and working from her parent's home. They provided her with a LINC computer and so she is considered to be the first user of a "Personal Computer" in her own home. Wilkes went on to develop more and more sophisticated programs, which became the building blocks of modern computers.

Eventually Wilkes left the computer world to pursue her original dream, and attended Harvard Law School. She was head of the Economic Crime and Consumer Protection Division of the Middlesex County District Attorney's Office, and went on to teach in the Trial Advocacy Program at Harvard Law School. Mary sat as a judge for competitions for law school students for 18 years. Eventually, her two worlds finally collided, and she sat as an independent person officially appointed to settle disputes, primarily on cases involving computer science and information technology.

"I'll bet you don't have a computer in your living room."

LYNN MARGULIS
BIOLOGIST

1938–2011

Lynn Margulis, an American biologist, is one of the most important women in the scientific understanding of evolution. In the 1970s, she presented a theory of evolution that explained how a new species may emerge. Although it was initially rejected, her ideas are now widely accepted.

ANCESTRAL HOST CELL

Born in Chicago, Lynn was highly educated, with a master's degree in zoology and genetics, and a PhD in genetics. She was married to the famous American astronomer Carl Sagan, though they divorced after having two children. Lynn then taught at Boston University for many years.

Her work focused on symbiosis—the concept that two organisms can either benefit or suffer from their relationship together. She is best known for her development of a theory that looked at the origin of cells, proposing that cells with a nuclei are the result of a mutually beneficial relationship between bacteria. She wrote about this in her book *Origin of Eukaryotic Cells*. Lynn also worked with the scientist James Lovelock, who proposed that Earth is a single organism, with all its elements relying on and affecting each other to keep a state of balance. She wasn't afraid to question controversial ideas within the scientific community, showing us how important it is to keep an open mind—there is still so much in science to discover!

MODERN CELL

"Life did not take over the world by combat, but by networking."

FLORENTINA MOSORA
Physicist and Actor

1940–1996

Florentina was born in Romania and, while in her twenties, worked as a film actress starring in many Romanian films, such as *Love at Zero Degrees* and *Under the Blue Arch*.

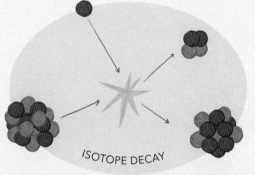

ISOTOPE DECAY

"Florentina Mosora was a perfectionist. She was an extraordinary co-worker, full of ideas ..."

MARCEL LACROIX

She went to university in Bucharest where she graduated from the Faculty of Physics. Florentina then moved to Belgium, where she worked on how to use stable isotopes in medicine. Stable isotopes do not decay, while unstable isotopes (which are radioactive) will decay into other elements. Unstable isotopes have been used in medicine for many years, treating diseases like cancer. Stable isotopes are now used in tests for liver function and nutrition.

She was awarded the 1979-1981 Prix Agathon de Potter for outstanding research work in physics by the Agathon de Potter Foundation at the Belgian Royal Academy. This allowed Florentina to have her research supported financially so that she could continue making discoveries that could help save lives. In 1989 she helped to organize a NATO workshop on the Biomechanical Transport Processes that happen within our bodies.

JOCELYN BELL BURNELL

ASTROPHYSICIST

1943–

Jocelyn Bell Burnell was born in Northern Ireland. Her father worked as an architect, and he helped design the Armagh Planetarium when Jocelyn was a child. During her visits she was encouraged to study astronomy by the scientists who worked there. However, her school didn't allow the girls to study science, they were only allowed to do cooking and knitting. Her parents protested, but eventually she transferred to another school where she was allowed to study physics.

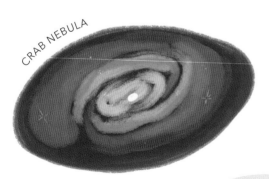

PULSAR STAR

the high-frequency fluctuations of radio sources, like stars. It can map the entire Northern sky in 24 hours.

One day, while working with the Array, Jocelyn noticed something that was not quite right. After lots of debate and research, she realized that it was not an anomaly—the signal was pulsing very regularly. She named it "Little Green Man 1" temporarily while they figured out what the source was. Eventually they figured out that it was a rapidly rotating neutron star, the collapsed core of a giant star. The "Little Green Man 1" then became known as a pulsar. It was the first of its kind to be discovered. The Nobel Prize in Physics in 1974 went to her graduate supervisors because, while Jocelyn

RADIO TELESCOPE

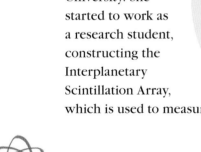

CRAB NEBULA

Jocelyn went on to study science at university and got her PhD degree from Cambridge University. She started to work as a research student, constructing the Interplanetary Scintillation Array, which is used to measure

"Minority folk bring a fresh angle on things and this is often a very productive thing. In general, a lot of breakthroughs come from the left field."

Bell Burnell made the discovery, she was only a research student at the time.

Since then, Jocelyn continues to do wondrous things. She has studied and taught at many universities across the world. Most recently she has been a professor of astrophysics at the University of Oxford in England, and in 2018 she became Chancellor of the University of Dundee. In the same year she was awarded the Special Breakthrough Prize in Fundamental

RADIO EMISSIONS EMITTED
BY A PULSAR STAR

Physics for her discovery of pulsars. It's the largest prize in science—she won US$3 million (£2.3 million)! Rather than keep the money for herself, Jocelyn did something wonderful. With the Institute of Physics, she is offering scholarships to research students from under-represented groups—women, ethnic minorities, refugees, and financially or educationally disadvantaged people. In doing so, she is paving the way for a new batch of talented physicists to emerge.

ROBERTA BONDAR
Zoologist and Astronaut

1945–

When Roberta was a child in Canada, her interest in science was so great that her dad built her a laboratory in their basement. She went on to study zoology and agriculture at university, followed by a Master of Science degree in experimental pathology. She finished academics with two doctorates in medicine and neuroscience.

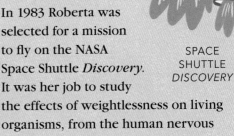

SPACE SHUTTLE *DISCOVERY*

In 1983 Roberta was selected for a mission to fly on the NASA Space Shuttle *Discovery*. It was her job to study the effects of weightlessness on living organisms, from the human nervous system to shrimp eggs.

After the successful conclusion of her mission as an astronaut, Roberta worked with NASA for more than a decade. She examined data brought back by astronauts, which has helped to understand the human body's ability to recover from time spent in space.

Aside from science, Roberta has pursued her interests in photography and has authored four books that feature her photographs of the Earth.

With her background and expertise as an astronaut, scientist. and natural photographer, Roberta has started her own charity, The Roberta Bondar Foundation. This is a non-profit organization that raises environmental awareness.

"When I was eight years old, to be a spaceman was the most exciting thing I could imagine."

SUN-YUNG ALICE CHANG
MATHEMATICIAN

1948–

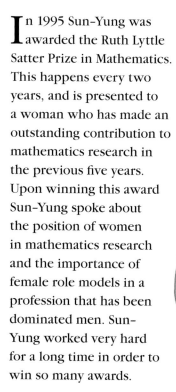

In 1995 Sun-Yung was awarded the Ruth Lyttle Satter Prize in Mathematics. This happens every two years, and is presented to a woman who has made an outstanding contribution to mathematics research in the previous five years. Upon winning this award Sun-Yung spoke about the position of women in mathematics research and the importance of female role models in a profession that has been dominated men. Sun-Yung worked very hard for a long time in order to win so many awards.

She was born in China, and went to university in Taiwan, where she received her bachelor of science degree. She received her PhD from the University of California, and on receiving her doctorate, Sun-Yung taught and worked as an assistant professor at many major universities throughout the United States. She did this all while pursuing her research interests of geometry and topology (the study of how an object behaves when it is twisted, stretched, or bent.)

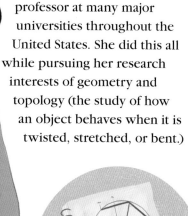

GEOMETRIC ANALYSIS

"In the mathematical community, we should leave room for people who want to do work in their own way. Mathematical research is not just as scientific approach; the nature of mathematics is sometimes close to that of art."

Sun-Yung then became a full professor at the University of California and Princeton University, where she teaches the next generation of great minds in mathematics.

SALLY RIDE

Astronaut

1951–2012

Sally Ride flew on the Space Shuttle *Challenger* in 1983, becoming the first American woman to go into space.

T-38 JET USED FOR TRAINING

Born in 1951 in California to well-educated parents, Sally briefly wanted to be a professional tennis player before deciding on a science career. She attended Stanford University, where she gained a very high level of education— two undergraduate degrees, a master's, and a doctorate in physics. She was selected by NASA to be one of the first-ever female astronauts after answering a newspaper advert.

NASA was looking for highly skilled people in technology and science. After her training, which included parachute jumping and water survival skills, her role was in communication. She became part of Space Shuttle's ground crew.

TENNIS RACKET

Her first foray into space itself, aboard *Challenger*, was during its seventh mission, when she was 32 years old. During this mission, she was the flight engineer. She became the first woman to control the Shuttle's robotic arm during an operation to deploy a communication satellite, as well as conducting other experiments. Before the launch it was reported that she was asked how she was going to wear makeup in space. She replied: "It's too bad this is such a big deal. It's too bad our society isn't further along." Sally was an amazing role model for women wanting to venture into space and have equal treatment as they do so.

Challenger broke apart 73 seconds into its flight. Sally helped investigate what went wrong and became involved in NASA's goal-setting for the future. She left NASA in 1987.

Sally became a professor of physics at the University of California. She also founded Sally Ride Science, a company with the aim of encouraging students to learn about science, and wrote a number of books for children.

> *"I didn't succumb to the stereotype that science wasn't for girls."*

THE NASA MAKEUP KIT

Her second *Challenger* flight came in 1984, again taking command of the robotic arm for adjustments to the craft. She would have entered space a third time, but the preparations were stopped after the tragedy in 1986, when

When reflecting on her time in space, she is quoted as saying that "on launch day, there was so much excitement and so much happening around us in crew quarters, even on the way to the launch pad, I didn't really think about it that much at the time—but I came to appreciate what an honor it was to be selected to be the first to get a chance to go into space."

She died of cancer in 2012, one of the few people to know the reality of what it is like to experience life outside of Earth.

ADRIANA OCAMPO
PLANETARY GEOLOGIST

JUNO
SPACECRAFT

1955–

Adriana Ocampo, from Colombia, now works for the European Space Agency (ESA) and specializes in studying Earth's terrain using remote-sensing equipment. She was one of the discoverers of the crater in Mexico that is thought to have been created by an enormous rock from space that hit Earth 65 million years ago. The impact perhaps sparked the extinction of the dinosaurs! Adriana also used instruments on craft sent into space, such as the *Juno* mission to Jupiter, to study other planets, moons, and comets in the solar system. She loved space from childhood, working at the Jet Propulsion Laboratory at NASA as a teenager, and then as a research scientist before moving to the ESA in the Netherlands.

CAROL SHAW
Video Game Designer

1955–

Carol Shaw was one of the first professional females working in the video game industry—an industry now worth more than US$100 billion. She always excelled at mathematics, and attended the University of California to study electrical engineering and computer science. She then began working at Atari, a pioneer company in the creation of gaming and home computers, as the only woman, releasing her game Tic-Tac-Toe. She also worked at a company called Tandem, and Activision, creating successful games such as River Raid and Happy Trails. She made enough money to stop working in her mid-thirties—an amazing achievement. Even though gaming is still dominated by male programmers, Carol was truly a trailblazer in this arena.

ATARI CONSOLE

PARAMJIT KHURANA
MOLECULAR BIOLOGIST

MULBERRIES

1956–

Paramjit Khurana, an Indian scientist, specializes in plant molecular biology and is a professor at the University of Delhi. Highly educated to PhD level in botany, Paramjit has made incredible contributions to farming, specifically her work with and understanding of wheat. She has been able to develop crops that can survive in all kinds of hostile weather conditions. The implications for this are huge, as farming communities operate in a far more sustainable and productive way, less susceptible to the elements. She has transformed the genetics of Indian wheat, mulberry, rice, and tomatoes in order to protect them from "stress" conditions such as drought.

MAE CAROL JEMISON
Engineer & Astronaut

1956–

ENDEAVOUR SHUTTLE

Mae Carol Jemison was the first female African-American astronaut to go into space. She also worked as a doctor, a volunteer for the Peace Corps, and is a founder of technology companies. In 1992 she climbed aboard the Space Shuttle *Endeavour* and went on an incredible journey that lasted eight days. As a space mission specialist, she was responsible for many experiments during the flight, including examining the effect of weightlessness and motion sickness on herself and the other astronauts. After leaving NASA, Mae founded a company that promoted advanced technologies. Her advice is inspirational: "Never be limited by other people's limited imaginations … If you adopt their attitudes, then the possibility won't exist because you'll have already shut it out."

FREDA MILLER
NEUROBIOLOGIST

1957–

CARDIAC CELLS

Freda Miller has spent her academic career studying neurobiology and now specialises in cell

LIVER CELLS

and molecular developmental neurobiology at The Hospital for Sick Children Research Institute.

Cell and molecular developmental neurobiology is the study of the nervous system at a very early stage of development. The development of the nervous system begins in the embryo's first few days, and it is one of the most complex processes for the body to undertake. Through Freda Miller's research the nervous system

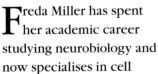

can be studied at a cellular level, meaning that we can understand more about brain illnesses and find out what causes them and how they can be cured or stopped.

STEM CELLS

Freda Miller does all of this while working as a professor at the University of Toronto, Canada, where she teaches bright young minds how to expand on her work, so that one day we might fully understand exactly how our bodies function.

BLOOD CELLS

"You change the world by educating one young mind at a time."

She has written more than 140 scientific papers, reviews, and book chapters, all so more people can have access to her extensive knowledge, benefit from it, and hopefully build upon it.

MUSCLE CELL

NERVE CELL

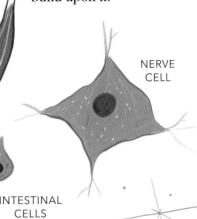
INTESTINAL CELLS

ELLEN OCHOA

Astronaut

1958–

Upon completing her training in 1991, Ellen Ochoa became the first Hispanic woman in the world to become an astronaut and be launched into space. Not just once—Ellen worked as a mission specialist and flight engineer on four space flights, logging 40 days spent in space. She even played her beloved flute on board the shuttle *Discovery*.

Ellen has worked extremely hard to get where she is now—the vice chairperson of the National Science Board, which runs the National Science Foundation. Prior to taking this position, Ellen was the first Hispanic, and second female, to become director of NASA's Johnson Space Center,

"Don't be afraid to reach for the stars. I believe a good education can take you anywhere on Earth and beyond."

after serving as deputy director for several years.

Before her appointment as a leader of NASA, she spent many years training and completing missions in space. From studying the Earth's ozone layer to executing the first docking to the International Space Station, her adventures in space were made possible due to her work as a research engineer. During that time she helped create several systems and methods that were awarded patents. She started out as a student, studying electrical engineering at Stanford University, and created a career that made her dreams come true!

DISCOVERY SHUTTLE

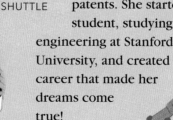

FLUTE PLAYED IN SPACE

CHIEKO ASAKAWA
Computer Scientist

1958–

Losing her sight as a young teenager led to Cheiko Asakawa finding her life's mission—making the web readily accessible for the visually impaired. She has made amazing developments in her field, including the creation of a voice-activated web browser and a form of digital braille. Her main concern is ensuring all people can use technology so they have equal opportunities, as it becomes an ever-increasing, integral part of life. She is now developing a system that will help blind people navigate indoors. Cheiko works for IBM, and was made a fellow of the company in recognition of her incredible work.

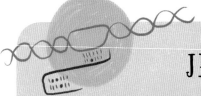

DNA WITH REPLACED
SEQUENCE OF INFORMATION

JENNIFER DOUDNA
BIOCHEMIST

1964–

Jennifer Doudna, an American biochemist, found her love of science as a child growing up surrounded by nature in the countryside of Hawaii. Today, she works as a professor of molecular and cell biology and chemistry at the University of Berkeley, and holds other prominent roles in the world of science. Her goal has been to understand how RNA molecules convert information in DNA. Alongside French microbiologist Emmanuelle Charpentier, she discovered a molecular tool known as CRISPR-Cas9. It is a powerful tool for editing genomes, the complete set of genes in a cell, which is a huge development in the treatment of genetic illnesses.

SUNITA WILLIAMS
Biochemist

1965–

ROBONAUT 2

Sunita Williams, a female American astronaut, has spent a vast amount of time in space—322 days! She worked on the International Space Station over two separate missions, carrying out much research and exploration, including with humanoid robots, and has served as both a flight engineer and commander. During her intensive training she had to learn to survive in the wild, and had to live underwater for nine days to prepare her for extreme conditions. She is the second woman on NASA's space endurance list for the amount of hours in space, and sixth overall. Sunita is now training for Boeing's new Starliner spacecraft, and a third mission to the International Space Station.

SUNETRA GUPTA
EPIDEMIOLOGIST

1965–

Sunetra Gupta, an esteemed scientist and novelist, studies the evolution of diversity in pathogens (microorganisms that can cause disease). She is particularly interested in discovering more about HIV, malaria, meningitis, and flu (influenza), and is a respected voice in the world of public health. Born in Calcutta, India, she spent much of her childhood in Africa, in Ethiopia and Zambia. She studied biology, yet is also heavily involved in the arts, with five successful novels to her name. Sunetra works as a Professor of Theoretical Epidemiology at the University of Oxford and is an avid supporter of female voices in science.

FLU VIRUS

EMMANUELLE CHARPENTIER
Microbiologist

1968–

GENE-EDITED
BUTTERFLY WINGS

Having studied microbiology (the branch of science that deals with microorganisms), and biochemistry (the study of chemical processes in living organisms), French scientist Emmanuelle Charpentier was able to make the discovery that she is best known for.

CRISPR-Cas9 (see page 118) has generated a lot of excitement in the science world because it is faster, cheaper, more accurate, and more efficient than any other existing technologies of its type. CRISPR-Cas9 is a method that allows scientists to edit the genes in a living organism's DNA!

Emmanuelle was able to decipher the molecular mechanisms of the bacteria and to repurpose it into a tool for editing genomes. This technology allows the bacteria to remember a virus, so if the virus attacks again, the CRISPR can target it and then use Cas9 to cut apart the virus's DNA, which will then disable it.

RNA CUTTING DNA

This technology is going a long way to preventing and treating diseases in humans, despite it being in its early stages.

It's no wonder that in Spring 2015 *Time* Magazine made Charpentier one of the 100 most influential people in the world.

"Basic research is essential for progress."

MAYLY SÁNCHEZ
Physicist

LABORATORY GAUGE

1972–

In order to understand the incredible work being done by Venezuelan Mayly Sánchez, we must first understand one of the most abundant particles in the universe. The neutrino is a subatomic particle, very similar to an electron, but it holds no electrical charge and almost no mass. They are so abundant because they barely react with any other matter, but as plentiful as the neutrino might be, they are very difficult to detect. What is known, is that they play a big part in discovering how the universe formed.

Conducting experiments to understand neutrinos and subsequently discover more about the universe is the reason why Mayly Sánchez is so important. Deservedly, she has been awarded the Presidential Early Career Awards for Scientists and Engineers, the highest accolade given to beginning scientists in the United States. She has also been named by the BBC as one of the top ten female scientists in Latin America.

Mayly is currently the spokeswoman for the Accelerator Neutrino Neutron Interaction Experiment (ANNIE) which will be the first test of new photodetection technology applied to neutrino detection.

WON PRESIDENTIAL EARLY CAREER AWARD FOR SCIENTIST AND ENGINEERS

"For contributions to the detection and study of neutrinos and their role in some of the most fundamental problems in physics, and for reaching out to potential women STEM majors and exciting them about opportunities in the STEM fields, in particular physics and astronomy."

PHOTODETECTION EQUIPMENT

LINDA NEDBALOVÁ
ANTARCTIC RESEARCHER

1976–

Linda Nedbalová was born in the Czech Republic in 1976 (when it was known as Czechoslovakia). Linda's schooling spanned through a lot of political changes. When she was born, it was a Communist country, but when she was 13 the Communist regime collapsed, and Czechoslovakia later became two separate states—Slovakia and the Czech Republic. Her home city of Prague was in the new Czech Republic and became the capital city.

"Algae are ... responsible for half of the photosynthesis that takes place on the planet and, because of that, the oxygen in every second breath we take."

PETER BICKERTON

seven years later, and now she teaches at the university as an assistant professor.

Linda is interested in studying the ecology of polar and mountain lakes (ecology is a branch of biology that looks at the relations and interactions between organisms and their environment). Her special interest is the algae and bacteria that live in these extreme habitats, as they are often the source of energy on which other life depends. Linda also spends her time looking at the diversity, ecology, and physiology of snow algae, as these groups of organisms can help us understand the mechanisms of cold adaptation and how we might apply it to many other aspects of our lives.

MOUNTAIN LAKE

Linda stayed in Prague and attended Charles University where she received a Master of Science degree in biology in 2000. She received her PhD there

Linda has been on two expeditions. With a fellow scientist, she has performed a pioneering

CYANOBACTERIA

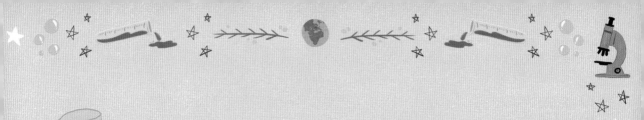

limnological survey (the study of inland water ecosystems). This survey has provided some very important results in the ecology of Antarctic bacteria and algae. Her studies were conducted in the Ulu peninsula of the James Ross Island, which holds the Mendel Polar Station (the first Czech Antarctic Base), and the Clearwater Mesa, an elevated area of land with a flat top and sides as steep as cliffs.

SNOW ALGAE

Linda won the Czech Republic's Academy of Sciences Award given to young researchers for outstanding achievements in 2011. With the work she is doing, who knows how many more awards she might go on to receive, and how many discoveries she has yet to make? The Antarctic is rich with uncharted ground and fresh snow. The science community will be keeping their eyes on Linda to see what she does in the future.

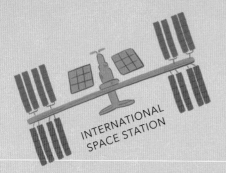

INTERNATIONAL SPACE STATION

YI SO-YEON
ASTRONAUT

1978–

In 2008, Yi So-yeon became the first South Korean to go into space. The Russian government flew her as a guest, and during her time in space she carried out scientific experiments while also communicating with the media back on Earth. She defied social conventions, stating that if women "can hear from their heart that they want to be an engineer or an astronaut," they should become one. One of her tasks was to monitor how a lack of gravity and a space environment affected fruit flies, while another was to study the effect of space travel on her own body; monitoring how it affected her heart, eyes, and even the shape of her face by taking photos to monitor swelling. Yi So-yeon also examined plant growth and weather storms on Earth.

NINA TANDON
Biomedical engineer

1980–

MODEL HEART

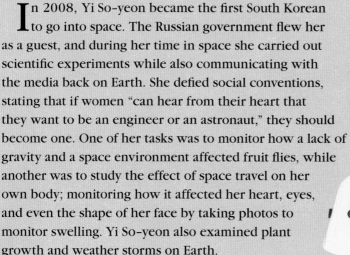

Nina Tandon is doing the work of the future, today. She is working to create a technology that would allow artificial hearts and bones to be grown in a lab and then put into bodies. She also is heavily involved in a new branch of mind-boggling biology—a world where cells are used to create new realities for products for humans. Some of her concepts are hard to imagine, but she is working on making them come true. Imagine a bridge that could repair itself in a similar way that the body heals after a cut. Her mind is incredible and she is at the forefront of a new wave of technological revolution. She is truly an inspiration to us all.

JOY BUOLAMWINI
COMPUTER SCIENTIST

FACIAL ANALYSIS

1990–

Joy Buolamwini is working at the forefront of computer science and artificial intelligence. She is particularly concerned with its potential pitfalls, particularly the dangers of facial analysis, delivering a TED talk on the topic. Joy herself founded the Algorithmic Justice League to try and challenge the inbuilt bias that occurs in the kind of software that makes decisions based on gender and racial appearances. Joy is actively involved in the development of science at the MIT Media Lab, a research lab at the Massachusetts Institute of Technology. She promotes youth engagement with science, particularly in Africa. She is an incredible inspiration to younger generations, who will grow up with an understanding that they are creators, not just consumers, thanks to the light-speed advancement of technology.

NAOMI WU
Engineer

OPEN-SOURCE SCREWDRIVER

1994–

Naomi Wu is an amazing example of a young woman pushing the boundaries of technology. A famous Chinese online personality, she uses her internet persona to challenge gender roles through media such as Twitter and YouTube. Naomi promotes a new wave of thinking and uses her gender to provoke conversation about the way women are viewed and judged by society in the workplace. She works in a highly male dominated world of STEM (science, technology, engineering, and mathematics) and in 2017 was celebrated as one of the most influential women in the world of 3-D printing. Much of her work is centred around "wearable technology" clothing or accessories that contain electronic devices.

GLOSSARY

ALGEBRA Working out equations using letters and symbols to represent numbers.

ALGORITHM A set of rules to solve a problem.

ANTHROPOLOGY The branch of science that studies the human race.

ASTRONOMY The branch of science that studies the universe beyond Earth.

ATMOSPHERE The layer of gases around a planet.

BIOCHEMISTRY A branch of science that studies chemical reactions in organisms.

CELL One of the tiny units from which all living things are made.

CHEMISTRY The science that studies the form and function of basic elements and their compounds.

CHROMOSOME The part of a cell that carries genetic information.

COSMOLOGY The science of the origin and development of the Universe.

CRYSTALLOGRAPHER Someone who studies atomic or molecular structures.

DISCRIMINATION When people are treated unfairly because of their age, gender, race, or sexuality.

DNA A complicated chain of chemicals inside each cell, giving each organism its special qualities.

EMPATHY The ability to understand or share someone else's feelings.

ETHOLOGIST Someone who studies how animals behave.

EVOLVE To gradually change and develop over time.

FEMINIST Someone who believes that people should be treated equally and have equal opportunities and rights, regardless of gender.

FORCE Energy that makes an object move.

GALAXY A system of millions of stars, gas, and dust held together by gravity.

GENES A combination of molecules that give a living thing its characteristics.

GENETICIST Someone who studies the process by which living organisms inherit traits and characteristics.

GRAVITY A force that pulls an object toward a larger object.

ISOTOPE Any of two or more atoms that have the same number of protons but differ in the number of neutrons.

MASS The amount of matter (stuff) that something is made of.

NEUROBIOLOGIST A scientist who researches the nervous system in animals and humans.

NEURON A specialist nerve cell that passes impulses.

ORBIT The curved path of an object around another object (like the Moon around the Earth).

ORGANISM An individual living thing.

PHILANTHROPIST Someone who supports charitable causes and donates generous sums of money to them.

PHYSICS The science that deals with matter and energy, their qualities, and the relationships between them.

PREHISTORIC Before written historical records.

PREJUDICE An opinion (often negative) that is formed without experience or knowledge.

PRIMATOLOGIST Someone who studies monkeys and apes.

PROTEIN A nutrient that is needed for growth and repair.

PSYCHOLOGIST A scientist who studies the human mind.

RADIATION A form of energy that can travel as rays or waves and is invisible to the human eye.

SCIENTIST A person who works in any branch of science.

SEGREGATION The separation by law of people according to their race.

TEMPERATURE The amount of heat energy present.

TISSUE A specific type of material that makes a living thing.

VACUUM A space with no particles (solid, liquid, or gas) in it.

VIROLOGIST A scientist who studies viruses.

WEIGHT The force exerted on a body by gravity.

X-RAYS Waves of energy that can pass through many materials.

INDEX